Sloops and Brigs

By the same author

The Frigates: an account of the lesser warships of the wars from 1793 to 1815

Sloops
and Brigs

An account of the smallest vessels of the Royal Navy
during the great wars 1793 to 1815

by James Henderson CBE

Drawings by Ernest E Yelf

Adlard Coles Limited   London

Granada Publishing Limited
First published in Great Britain 1972 by Adlard Coles Limited
3 Upper James Street London W1R 4BP

© Estate of James Henderson 1972

ISBN 0 229 98644 7
Printed in Great Britain by
Willmer Brothers Limited Birkenhead

Dedicated to the 20,000 men who served in
the Light Coastal Forces during the War
from 1939 to 1945, of whom scarcely one in
twenty was of the regular Royal Navy;
who manned over 1500 ships of under
100 tons, and fought in 782 engagements;
and in salutation to the complements
of the 176 light craft which failed to report

Contents

Plates

Notes on the plates are on pages 173 to 175

Author's Notes

To avoid any possible confusion, the name of every ship under British command is printed in SMALL CAPITALS; the names of ships of all other nations are printed in *italics*.

Dates are given fully and frequently, to avoid the annoyance of having to turn back to remind oneself. Naval accounts are very liable to be short of full dates, as the ships' logs of the period showed the day of the month, but named the month only on the 1st, and the year only on 1st January.

Facing forward in a ship, the starboard side is on the right hand; that on the left is now called port, but until well into the nineteenth century it was called larboard; the contemporary expression of larboard is used here, as there is no possibility of confusion in writing.

At that period, every officer commanding a warship, however small, was always called 'Captain' on all occasions. All sloops and lesser ships were however captained by a commander or lieutenant, who reverted to his substantive rank immediately he ceased to command the ship. A post captain, commanding a ship of 20 guns nominal or larger, was a captain for life, until he attained flag rank or committed some such fault that he was dismissed the service. He could not be reduced in rank. In this book every officer is called by his substantive rank, to avoid any confusion between the lordly captain of a 74 and the humble lieutenant who was nevertheless 'Captain' of a 70-ton schooner.

The modern yachtsman is accustomed to think of a 'sloop' as a small single-masted vessel of simple cutter rig, usually Bermuda type. At the time of which we write, however, a sloop was a full-rigged ship of 300 to 400 tons, the largest which could be commanded by an officer of less rank than post Captain.

Sloops and Brigs

1

The Ships

A great fleet is sailing down the Channel. Standing on Beachy Head, you can see neither the van nor the rear, for it stretches over sixty miles of sea, and with a fair wind will take a long summer's day to pass. The fleet is all small vessels, although it includes tall three-masted full-rigged ships as well as two-masted brigs and single-masted cutters. These are the little ships which Britain sent out to war against the French Republic and against Napoleon; ships too small to be 'rated', too small to be commanded by a post captain; but each with a purpose, each with a duty, and many of them to perform astounding feats of naval warfare. If you wait long enough, perhaps you will see a much smaller fleet returning; for of seven hundred ships sent out, more than three hundred failed to report.

In the earlier wars of the eighteenth century and the later seventeenth, the emphasis was on the line of battle; there was little use for a ship which could not 'lie in the line' except to carry despatches. At the great battle off the Gunfleet Sand in 1666 both the British and the Dutch deployed almost a hundred battleships apiece, three times as many as fought at Trafalgar. In the Republican and Napoleonic wars the British line of battle rarely exceeded a hundred ships altogether, and only six times in the more than twenty years of war was there a fleet engagement; the rest of the time the great ships were wearily blockading the French fleets in their various ports – fleets far too powerful to be let loose, which by their mere presence in their harbours as 'a fleet in being' immobilised the battle strength of the Royal Navy. The active part of the war was to be carried out by the smaller rated ships, the frigates, whose work I have elsewhere described, and by the light vessels, the unrated, the sloops and brigs.

This deployment of the little ships was made possible by a remarkable step in naval gunnery, the invention of the carronade. This was designed by General Robert Melville, and the first was cast at the Carron works in Scotland, near Falkirk, in 1779. This was of enormous bore, a 68-pounder, but in practice it was found that the 32-pound shot, the heaviest thrown by the long guns of the largest ships, would smash through any timber that could be built into a ship. A few 68-pounders were issued to very large ships, to be loaded with one round shot and a keg of 500 musket balls, chiefly to deter boarders; the first shot fired by VICTORY at Trafalgar was exactly this, smashing through the cabin of the *Bucentaure* with devastating effect. Ships of the line and frigates were given a few carronades for their upperworks, but most of the little ships were completely re-armed, if their construction was suitable. The enhancement of force was extraordinary. The 18-gun ship-sloop had formerly carried just that number of 6-pounders on her main deck, her upperworks being unarmed except for muskets; now she carried 18 carronades, 32-pounders, on her main deck, and six carronades, 18-pounders, on her forecastle and quarter-deck, along with two long 6-pounders as bow and stern chasers. This gave her a broadside twice as heavy as that of a 32-gun frigate of twice her tonnage.

There were of course some snags; the range of the carronade, half a mile, was only half that of a long gun; but then most actions took place inside two hundred yards. Carronades were liable to overheat, recoil too violently, over-turn, or break the tackle which fastened them to the ship's side; but all these risks could be accepted in return for a quadrupling of the fighting force of the vessel. Sloops and brigs could now undertake convoy duties, and not only beat off the French privateers which swooped out from that coast, but also pursue them among the shoals and reefs of their harbourages, where heavier vessels could not venture. They could be consort to long-gun ships; for example, when the frigate PHOEBE sailed to the South Pacific to search for the American frigate *Essex* she was accompanied by the ship-sloop CHERUB, invaluable for nosing into ill-chartered harbours, and able to account for herself in the final engagement. Many sloops were used on the East Indies station, sounding into little-known coasts in advance of the heavier ships.

The big ships of the Royal Navy were almost all built in the Royal Dockyards, which alone had the facilities for dealing with ships of 2,000 tons; but of the unrated ships few exceeded 400 tons, well within the capacity of most shipyards building merchantmen, and the majority were built by contract; as the Navy could not spare any experienced officers to 'stand by' a small ship in building, a good deal had to be left to the honesty of the contractor, which was not always impeccable. Most of the small ships for the East India station were built at Bombay, under the supervision of the Honourable Company, thus saving the long voyage round the Cape in a small vessel which could not carry water and provision for the voyage without putting in somewhere. These were mostly teak-built, a splendid sea timber, but open to one objection : in action most wounds were by splinters, and a splinter wound from teak was almost sure to go septic. For the North American station, many of the smaller ships were built in Bermuda, of the local cedar, a wood very soft but very durable; it had the advantage that shot would usually go through it without scattering deadly splinters all around.

There was an apparent anomaly connected with the intro-duction of the carronade : it was never included in the stated force of a warship. Thus a 36-gun frigate remained a 36, although she would in fact mount 10 carronades, doubling her weight of broadside; and an 18-gun sloop remained an 18-gun sloop, even if she were armed with 26 heavy carronades. There was reason of a sort behind this: a ship of twenty guns or over had to be commanded by a post captain, and there just wasn't room on the captains list for all the commanders of sloops as well. Moreover, the pay and privileges of most of the officers depended on the rating of their ship. The whole system was ultimately reformed, but not until after the end of the wars.

Tables are rather dreary, especially for those who compile them; but a glance at Table I will give a picture of the little-ship Navy, at the beginning and end of the wars; beginning with 52 ships and ending, after all losses, with 339 in full commission. The first class, the quarter-decked ship-sloop, only began building after the first war started, but there were 33 when the wars ended. With the formidable armament already described they were effective ships of war, and there were few squadrons which did not have at least one of them. Some, such as the ARROW and the DART, were far more powerful than rated ships commanded by post captains, but sloops they remained, and we shall hear more about them. The disadvantage of these sloops was that they could not carry provisions and water for very long voyages without calling in somewhere for supplies, thus giving away their location; so that for inter-ocean passages they were usually attached to a frigate or squadron, from which they could draw stores. The flush-decked ships could carry only their rated number of guns, and these were usually left as 6-pounder long guns.

The brig-sloop was a two-masted square-rigged vessel, so handy for all sorts of odd jobs that we begin with less than 15 and finish with more than 150. They could carry no more than their rated guns, 6-pounders in the 18-gun class and 4-pounders in the others; but quite a number were armed with 18- and 24-pound carronades. The 18-gun brig-sloops were quite as powerful as the 18-gun flush-decked ship-sloops, which they superseded, being handier in every way and requiring less

18 *Sloops and Brigs*

crew. Their later armament was sixteen 32-pounder carronades and two long 6s as chase guns, a formidable force. The stores question limited their range, and most of the British-built brigs were used in European waters, while locally-built brigs were used on the American and East Indian stations; but they were quite capable of sailing anywhere in the world as long as they could get supplies.

The bomb-ketch was a very specialised ship, of odd appearance, like a sloop with its foremast removed and its mainmast greatly enlarged. The space between the mainmast and the bowsprit was given over to the two mortars, one 11-inch and one 13-inch, mounted on special decks stuffed up with cut lengths of old rope to lessen the effect of the recoil on the ship's timbers. The forestays of the huge mainmast were made of iron chain, because of the great flash upwards when the mortars were fired. The mortars were fixed, and the only way of using them was to moor the ship with springs on the cables, and swing the ship with these until the mortars were more or less in the line wanted. Range was adjusted by the amount of gunpowder – 'Another half-shovel, there!' The bursting charge was set off by a fuse, which could be adjusted in length; when loading, the fuse was downwards, so as to be ignited by the discharge. The idea of pitching large explosive bombs at a high angle into otherwise impregnable positions was quite a good one, but it was seldom successful. For one thing, though the 11-inch mortar was reliable enough, the 13-inch usually split after less than twenty shots. The other armament of the bomb-ketch consisted of eight guns abaft the mainmast, at first 6-pounder long guns, later 24-pounder carronades. On account of this not very formidable battery bomb-ketches were often used for convoy and other duties for which they were not designed. As they had to be very strongly built to take the kick of the mortars, after the wars were over they were used by Admiralty for Arctic exploration – HECLA, EREBUS and TERROR being the most famous.

Anything smaller than a bomb-ketch was not commanded by a Commander but by a Lieutenant, a distinction to which we shall revert later. Gun-brigs were much smaller than brig-sloops, and the only class of any importance was the 12-gun brig, of which there were 67 at the end of the wars; originally intended for 4-pounder long guns but soon mounting 18-pound carronades, with a complement of about 50 men and boys. These light vessels were mostly used on Baltic convoys, and suffered a lot of rough handling from the Danish rowing gun-boats, well-armed and well-manned, equally competent in calms or squalls.

The schooners and cutters were mostly employed in carrying despatches – *avisos* the Spaniards called them. The largest class was the 10-gun cutter, of which we find 24 at the close of play. One or more were attached to every fleet, but they were not expected to take part in a fleet action – indeed, the fore-castle carronades of a ship of the line would have shattered any of them into flinders. Their duty was to hang about on the fringe of the battle making observations, repeating signals, and afterwards to carry the despatches home. Thus the little schooner PICKLE, Lieutenant Lapenotiere, brought home Collingwood's despatches after Trafalgar, having taken no part in the fighting; but she was present, and the lieutenant received a hundred-guinea sword from Lloyd's Patriotic Fund, like every other captain of a ship in the action. The general idea was that these small ships, being fore-and-aft rigged, could lie at least a point nearer the wind than any square-rigged ship, and could therefore dodge any powerful interception; a theory which quite frequently worked.

The smallest class of all was the 4-gun schooner, about 75 tons, with a complement of about 20 men and boys. These were built at Bermuda of the local cedar, an excellent timber for the purpose; originally they carried 4-pounder long guns, later 12-pounder carronades. These vessels have been much decried by early naval writers as being too small for any real fighting, crank, liable to overset, bad sailers, etc; but it is impossible to believe that the expert Bermudan shipbuilders could build so badly ships of a size and type to which they were so well accustomed. Much more probably the crews and officers, trained in square-riggers, could not well handle the unfamiliar Bermudan rig; also they were liable, through ignorance, to be sent out in the hurricane season. They were intended mainly to seek out the nests of pirates which still infested the Caribbean seas, and would no doubt have been more successful if manned by Bermudans; but the canny islanders had more profitable employment elsewhere. As for size, it is worth remembering that in the Second World War the Royal Navy built more than 1,500 ships of less than 75 tons, with complements of less than 20 men, almost all RNVR or HO. Those tiny warships with their amateur crews made a notable contribution to the history of the Royal Navy.

Key to rig drawings

1 Fore royal	22 Fore mast
2 Main royal	23 Main mast
3 Mizzen royal	24 Mizzen mast
4 Fore topgallant	25 Bowsprit
5 Main topgallant	26 Jib-boom
6 Mizzen topgallant	27 Gaff topsail
7 Fore topsail	28 Lateen mizzen sail
8 Main topsail	29 Jib
9 Mizzen topsail	30 Dipping lug foresail
10 Foresail	31 Jigger
11 Mainsail	32 Chain mainstay
12 Driver	33 Position beyond for
13 Flying jib	mortars
14 Outer jib	34 Spritsail yard
15 Inner jib	35 Mainsail boom
16 Fore topgallant mast	36 Foresail boom
17 Main topgallant mast	37 Square topsail
18 Mizzen topgallant mast	38 Jigger boom
19 Fore topmast	39 Staysail
20 Main topmast	40 Mizzen sail
21 Mizzen topmast	

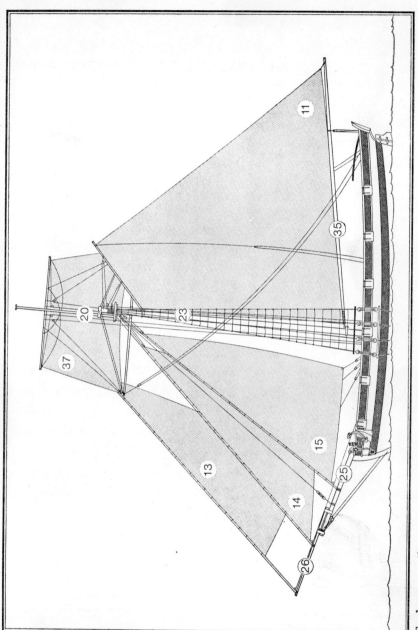

Twelve gun cutter

Eighteen gun (actual) brig-sloop

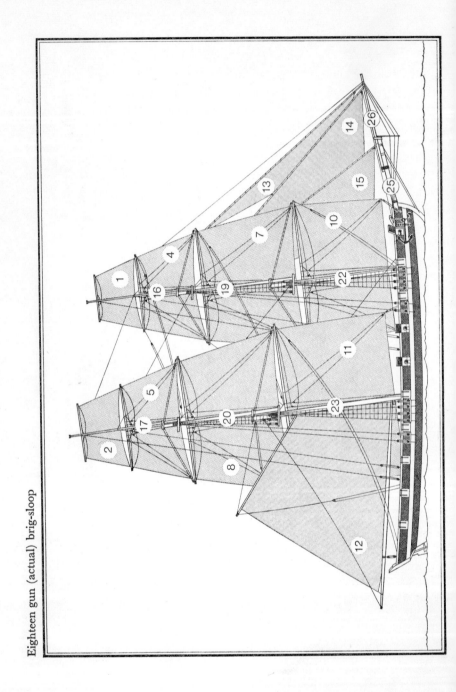

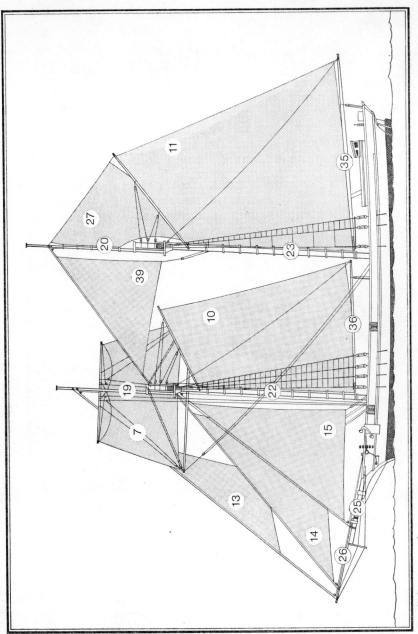

Small four-gun schooner

Eighteen gun (nominal) ship-sloop

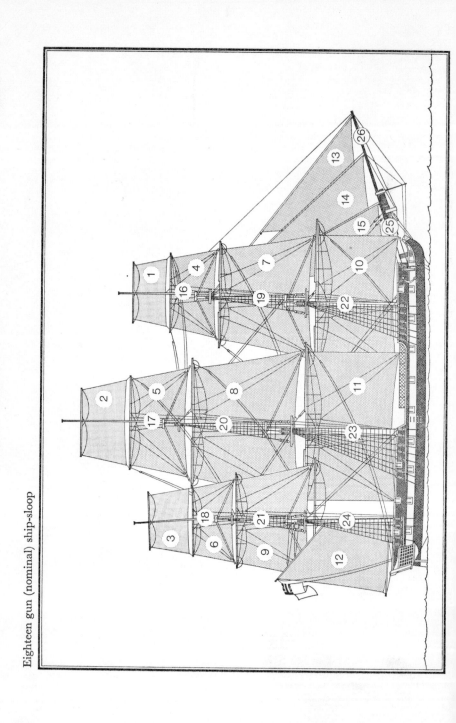

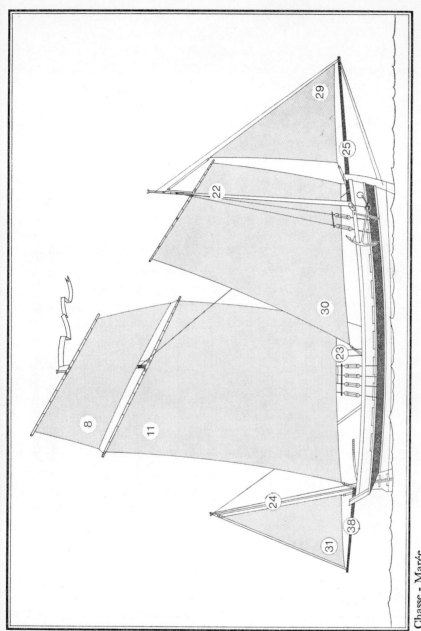

Chasse - Marée

Bark similar to WOLVERINE

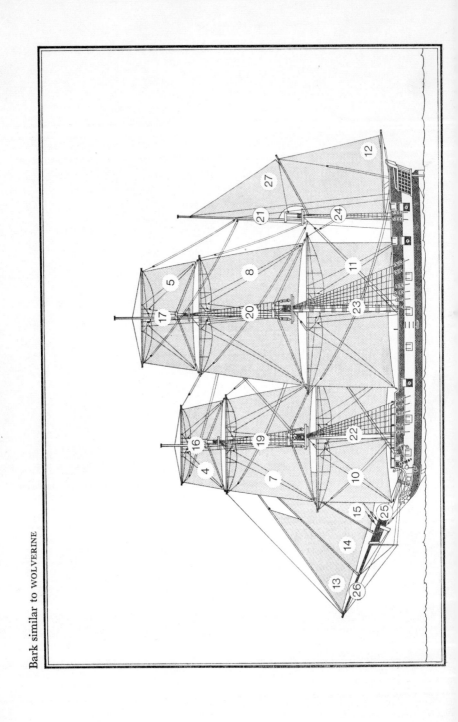

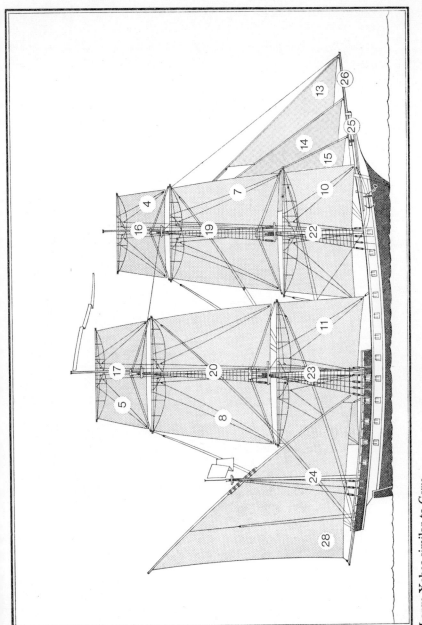

Large **Xebec** similar to *Gamo*

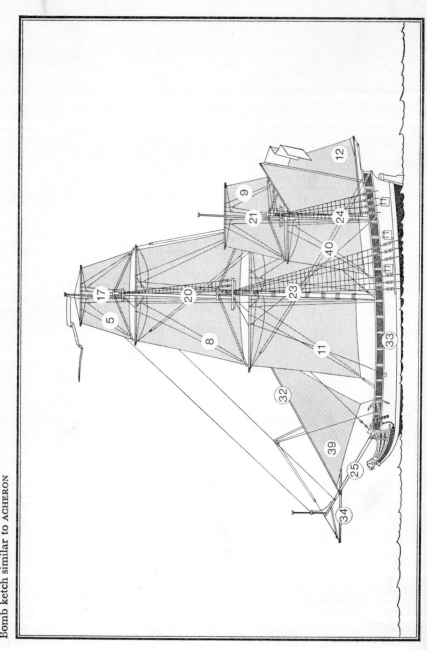

Bomb ketch similar to ACHERON

2

The Men

'There are no bad soldiers – only bad officers.' The old maxim was especially to be regarded in the case of the small ships, where a few men had to live for many months jammed together in inescapable proximity. The officer had to preserve at all times a strict and steady discipline; he had to keep his crew healthy and, if possible, happy; their morale and training high; and meanwhile he had to live almost among them, except that he had the after end of the deck and a dog-kennel of a cabin to which he could retreat. How were such officers selected?

The promotion system of the Georgian Navy was quite different from that of today; influence, then called 'interest' was essential. This is not to say that influence is not useful even in the modern Navy, where it is often necessary to choose one out of ten for a desirable posting; but there are no more post captains of eighteen years of age. Such great commanders as Pellew, Rainier and Nelson quite brazenly used their influence to have their relatives promoted post captain without any evidence whatever of their fitness for command. The reason was the system of promotion: below post captain there was no certainty whatever; once on the captains' ladder, promotion was by seniority *only*. Whether employed or on half pay, the captain went up through the captains list and through the flag officers list by survival only; only death or disgrace could knock him off the ladder. Thus if Nelson's uncle had not been Comptroller of the Navy he would not have been 'made post' at twenty, and therefore would not have been Rear-Admiral in time to have commanded the fleet at the Nile, nor Vice-Admiral in time to have been Commander-in-Chief, Mediterranean, at Trafalgar. This pressure by the influential to have their protegés pushed forward early meant of course that many able officers without such influence were kept back, and might even spend their whole naval career in the rank of midshipman; although, to the credit of Admiralty, such were usually promoted to lieutenant before retirement, so that they might have at least, for life, the half pay of that rank; there was nothing at all for midshipmen.

Sloops and brigs were too small to be commanded by a post captain; but the very smallest could be commanded only by a commissioned officer, which at that time meant a lieutenant; and for bomb-ketches and above, an appointed commander. There were two main streams from which such officers were fished: 'fortune's favourites' and 'the plodders'. The first class fell into two tributaries: those who had enough 'interest' to be brought into the flag-ship of the Commander-in-Chief of the station, which would carry eight lieutenants and up to twenty midshipmen, of approved social status; and the hero type. It became customary, after a well-fought and successful engagement, to promote the first lieutenant of each ship engaged to commander. These two sub-classes of 'fortune's favourites' were the more usual commanders of the larger sloops and brigs, not for long as a rule, because they flashed on to post rank after any kind of meritorious service. In the class-conscious society of that period, command sat more easily on the shoulders of gentlemen of good birth and breeding. The 'plodders', on the other hand, had nothing but capability and zeal to offer, and their promotion was slow. This hope deferred, which maketh the heart sick, had different effects on different men. Consider the two most famous 'plodders', who flourished a little before our period.

James Cook was well known in the Navy as the most competent hydrographer, cartographer and astronomer in the service, who had done much to make possible the taking of Quebec in 1759; but at forty years of age he was still a warrant officer, as sailing master, when in 1768 he was commissioned lieutenant in order to command the armed merchantman ENDEAVOUR on a scientific expedition to the South Seas. For his second great voyage he was promoted commander, so that he might command the sloop-of-war RESOLUTION on a similar exploration. As a reward he was made post captain in 1775 at the age of 47, and for his last voyage was in RESOLUTION with another sloop-of-war under his command. Thus the greatest of all navigators had never a larger command than a couple of 300-tonners, but this had no effect on his temper or spirits; he knew he was performing a great service, which nobody else could do so well, and it was the service that mattered. When he was murdered at Hawaii, his Lieutenant King, who continued his narrative, wrote:

> Thus fell our great and excellent commander.... How sincerely his loss was felt and lamented by those who had so long found their general security in his skill and conduct, and every consolation in their hardships in his tenderness and humanity, it is neither necessary nor possible for me to describe; much less shall I attempt to paint the horror with which we were struck, and the universal dejection and dismay which followed so dreadful and unexpected a calamity.

A notable epitaph, and from a shipmate.
The other 'plodder', for contrast, was William Bligh, who had sailed round the world with Cook and was promoted lieutenant in 1787, at the age of thirty-three, in order to command the armed transport ship BOUNTY, for a single purpose of transporting specimens of the breadfruit tree to the West Indies. He made the little ship of 215 tons an absolute hell for his crew, who, as is very well known, mutinied and turned him off in the

C

ship's launch, with the eighteen men, almost all officers or petty officers, who stood to their orders. The voyage they made, of 3,618 nautical miles to Timor, stands as one of the great sagas of the sea, and Bligh comes very well out of this; but when Government sent out a frigate to Tahiti and caught ten of the mutineers to bring home for trial, they all insisted that it was his brutal tyranny that had caused the mutiny, not the attractions of the Tahitan *vahinas*; and indeed Cook touched four or five times at Tahiti without a single desertion. It is interesting that one of the mutineers remarked that Bligh was no better born than any of themselves; they *preferred* the class system. They were all hanged, of course; but it is worth remarking that much later, when Bligh was Governor of New South Wales, he was deposed and imprisoned by the unanimous decision of the *military* officers on the station, because of his sadistic brutality. There was another William Bligh also a captain, and their naval nicknames are of interest: one was called 'Breadfruit Bligh', and the other 'Gentleman Bligh'.

Here we have two very different results of late promotion of really able men, philanthropist and misanthrope; no doubt the majority of the 'passed-overs' fell between these, concealing their disappointment and forbearing to revenge themselves on those under their command. It was with such that the smallest ships were usually officered; so many were being built that a great number of half-pay lieutenants had to be given the opportunity of a command, however small. Admirals usually preferred the older officers for such jobs as carrying despatches; they could be trusted to carry out their instructions with accuracy, not going out of the way to seek a brush with the enemy.

The largest sloops carried a fairly full complement of officers and men, not far short of that of a small frigate, which had twice the tonnage, so that quarters were close, very close. In addition to the commander, there were usually in the wardroom two lieutenants, lieutenant of Marines, sailing master, purser and surgeon; elsewhere were the standing warrant officers, the gunner, boatswain and carpenter, who remained more or less permanently with the ship whether in commission or not, having their families living on board when she was under repair or 'in ordinary'. These were appointed by Admiralty Warrant, and could not be disrated by the commander. Lesser warrant officers were the sergeant of Marines, the sailmaker, the master-at-arms, and the armourer. All of these petty officers had one or more mates, who berthed with the rest of the crew forward; then the cook and his mates, very important, the commander's steward and coxswain, and the wardroom stewards, who were usually youngsters. The Marines, usually about twenty, were berthed between the crew and the officers' quarters, in case of mutiny by night. The forward quarters were very tight indeed; it was quite impossible for the whole of the crew to sleep at the same time, but of course the exigencies of the service required that the crew be divided into two watches, four hours on and four hours off, except for the short dog watches, 4 to 6 p.m. and 6 to 8 p.m., which ensured that each watch was on a different time every day. Some captains tried a three-watch system, and even a quarter system, but these do not appear to have been successful, probably because of the difficulty of bringing in the dog watches, which were popular with everybody; hammocks were not slung, and the watch below could 'make do and mend' or get convivial on the rum ration, which was issued at noon as a rule.

Discipline in close quarters is always difficult, and depends very much on the personality of the commander. So far as his officers went, he was lacking the awful gulf which divided the post captain of a frigate from his lieutenants, as well as the superior accommodation and the certainty of flag rank on suvival. 'Fortune's favourites' had seldom any difficulty; they were usually young men of rank and education, obviously on the way up, and their 'interest' might be of the greatest in years to come. The 'plodders' found it more difficult, but experienced and good-natured officers could command their men as well as Cook. Others tried to maintain their command by severity, sometimes degenerating into sadism, and this was the reason for the few mutinies. It will be seen on Table II that two sloops were lost by the crew mutinying and taking the ship into an enemy harbour (a 10-gun cutter in 1797 and a 14-gun brig-sloop in 1800); nothing like the frightful mutiny of the frigate HERMIONE, which I have described elsewhere, but all due to the same cause – excessive and unreasonable use of the lash. It is significant that at no time during the long wars did any enemy ship come in through the mutiny of her crew. French agents spread the news through the British fleets that there was no flogging in the French Navy, which was true, and it took some time for the sailors to discover that the French equivalent for fifty lashes was seven years in the galleys, which meant hard labour, mostly on road construction, with a 24-pound shot chained to one ankle.

Flogging was always a serious matter. Only the captain could order it, although if it were recommended by a lieutenant he would have little alternative. All hands were mustered to witness punishment and it had to be noted in the ship's log, which had to be handed into Admiralty at the conclusion of the commission. Admiralty were well aware of the chief reason for mutiny and desertion, and it became known that logs were being scrutinised for punishments. During the short-lived Peace of Amiens half the Navy was put 'in ordinary' and its officers on half pay ashore; and when it came to re-commissioning, those who had acquired a reputation as floggers tended to be overlooked. Some were given command of convict hulks; some, like Bligh, were given charge of convict settlements as far away as possible; some were left on the beach. The Nelson school encouraged officers to keep up morale by example rather than by terror. Flogging was retained in all its terrors, and indeed it is difficult to imagine what sanction could have taken its place in the circumstances; but it was used with discretion, and there was no more mutiny and much less desertion. All the officers, of course, had been thoroughly birched at school, with a severity now incredible. With the spread of education all corporal punishment was discouraged, and when the Navy became a full-time well paid and pensioned career for ratings as well as officers, flogging was out: a dishonourable discharge was a much more severe penalty.

The very smallest ships, of under 100 tons and with fewer than 30 men, were not so completely officered; the lieutenant in command had another junior lieutenant, for there must always be two commissioned officers however small the vessel, but they had to do their own navigation, for a sailing master could not be spared. Boatswain, carpenter and cook were there, with their mates, leaving little more than 20 men and boys to work the ship and the guns. With a well-conditioned lieutenant in command and competent crew the atmosphere might have resembled that of a rather formal yachting party; but with a martinet in command and a tough boatswain trying to make seamen out of the sweepings of the receiving ships the little ship might be a little hell for everybody. The lieutenant commanding the smallest cutter was just as much an absolute monarch as the captain of a ship of the line, and had far fewer witnesses to restrain him.

The officers and petty officers were all volunteers who intended to make the Royal Navy a career for life. Not so with the ratings. There were a few in every ship who were volunteers, many joining through the Marine Society. This was founded in 1756 by Jonas Hanway (of umbrella fame) and had two main functions; it took in waifs and strays, many of them petty criminals, washed them, gave them some rudiments of education, and as the Navy required, passed them in with a good suit of clothes; on the other side, they took in men who were not seamen but were willing to volunteer (mostly because they were in some trouble or other), gave them some elementary maritime instruction, and passed them into the Navy as required, clean and clad. Marine Society men and boys were very welcome on board as a rule; they took a lot of training, but they were usually willing enough; they could stand the rough, tough life, for they had seldom known anything better and had seldom before been sure of their next meal; and they were unlikely to desert, for they had nowhere to go.

The majority of the men, however, were 'pressed' or picked up by the press-gang, that *very* rough and ready form of conscription. The common idea of its roughness is, however, greatly exaggerated, quite often by maritime novelists who knew better but wanted colour, 'Roderick Random' for example. The press-gang had to be commanded by a lieutenant, usually with a boatswain's mate; there were enough men with cudgels to discourage resistance, and four men with cutlasses beside the lieutenant; and all these men had to be really trustworthy, for they had every opportunity to desert. They could only press men 'using the sea', and who had used it for more than the preceding two years. They could not take any merchant service officer, boatswain or carpenter, any person (seaman or no) engaged in harvesting. Fishermen were usually exempt, although at times the needs of the Navy were allowed to outweigh the necessity of the food supply; and they could not touch a 'gentleman', a term capable of a wide interpretation. There is no doubt, however, that frequently a 'mistake' was made, and a stout young labourer or artisan was whisked away, and would be a thousand miles at sea before his relatives could get the ponderous machinery of the law in motion for his recovery.

All this was not enough to man the Navy, and in 1795 the Quota Acts were passed, whereby each town and county was required to produce a quota of 'volunteers', to the amount of roughly $\frac{1}{2}$ per cent of the population. The selection was entrusted to the justices of the peace, all estimable gentlemen, who found this a God-sent opportunity to get rid of their undesirables. The bounty was quite high – £70 – which gave offence to the volunteers of 1793, who had received £5. Apart from clearing off poachers, tramps and beggars, the debtors prisons were examined, where lay many a man for debts of less than £70. Put him in the quota, impound his bounty to pay his debts, and you are doing good all round. Except to the

Navy: these scrapings of the debtors prisons were usually quite unfit for seamen; they had usually some sort of education, had at some time been accustomed to home comforts, and hated everything about their position on the lower deck. It is not too sweeping to say that in almost every mutiny, large or small, a quota-man from a debtors prison would be found somewhere at the root of it. There was really no place for such men on a ship, and they were usually relegated to the most menial tasks, such as deck-swabbing and cleaning the 'heads', thus increasing their resentments. The quota was a drastic error: it would have been far better to have had fewer ships, all manned with 'prime seamen'.

The pay was certainly little attraction to so hard a life: an able seaman received 24s per month of four weeks at the beginning of the wars, and 33s 6d at the end, and had to find himself in clothes; but then he had lodgings of a sort, and the food was ample, although coarse and monotonous; and the drink! A gallon of beer per day was the ration, plus a rum issue of half a pint, so strong as to be almost pure alcohol. Admiral Vernon had been nicknamed 'Old Grog' because of the grogram coat he always wore; appalled at the consequences of issuing this firewater, when he was First Lord he decreed that this must be cut down with four times as much water, hence the mixture was called grog. Thus diluted, the daily ration was equal to little less than two bottles of rum at 70° proof. Admiral of the Fleet Lord Keith thought that almost every naval offence except theft arose from drunkenness; he emphasised the difference between a ship's company in the morning and in the afternoon. He felt that no more essential service could be rendered to the nation than to reduce the rum ration, but sadly concluded that it was not expedient during a war. In fact it was 1824 when the ration was cut. It is undoubtedly the case that at sea one can safely consume quantities of rum which would paralyse a city dweller, but eight pints of strong beer and nearly two bottles of rum would nowadays be considered the consumption of a hopeless alcoholic, not of a seaman who might be at any time called upon to go aloft in a storm. Still, alcohol was the only amelioration of their hard lives, and Keith was right to advise postponement. To cut the expected issue for 120,000 men in the time of war was to risk a general mutiny; with 20,000 in time of peace it was a risk which could be accepted.

The other great inducement was prize-money. The Government gave to the ship's company the full value of every prize, ship and cargo. Cases are recorded of lucky captains getting £40,000 and more in a day. Of course the seamen got nothing like that, but in such an action each man would get at least enough to set him up in a cosy little pub ashore. Such great prizes were rare, but they had existed, and as the pools competitor feels, it might be mine next time. It was sound policy of Admiralty to be so generous with prizes: the possibility of making oneself comfortable for life was much better *pour encourager les autres* than shooting Admirals. The biggest prizes fell to frigates, but a little brig, sent to harass the enemy's coastal trade, could send in as prizes dozens of well-laden coasters, as many as she could find prize crews for. Even a little 4-gun schooner had complete command over an unarmed freighter, and there were fewer to share the prize-money. There was plenty of speculation, of course, and prize agents and prize court officials became extremely rich. However, one must accept that 'where the carcase is, there will the vultures be gathered together', and it is unlikely that all the fingers in the prize-bowl, legal or otherwise, scooped out a greater percentage than, for example, an agent for a modern pop group.

Most people loathe statistics because they introduce fact where fancy loves to dwell. The popular idea is of fierce and bloody contests, in which all the casualties of the navy occurred. Fierce and bloody contests there were, but the casualties were only a small percentage of the actual losses in men: in fact negligible, so far as deaths were concerned.

Desertion was undoubtedly the largest single cause of loss of manpower. Samples taken at various periods show a fairly steady desertion rate of 500 a month, which does not appear an alarming drain on an establishment which at times amounted to 140,000 seamen and Marines; but it gives a total loss by desertion for the whole period of the two wars of more than 100,000 men – at least equal to, and probably more than, all the deaths in the service over the same period, from whatever cause. During the period of the war with the United States it was stated that 40,000 British deserters were serving in the American Navy; ten or so years later Admiralty in a more objective report estimated the number at 20,000. One figure seems too high, the other perhaps rather low; in the 'science' of statistics a good deal depends on what you are trying to prove at the time. In the first case, the point made was that the American Navy existed by tempting British sailors into that service; in the second case, the point to be made is that the loyal British tars loved the Navy so much that only 20,000 deserted to the Americans. Even taking the lower figure, it showed a pretty poor state of affairs, especially as the largest category of deserters was that of able seamen. The usual point of desertion was an American, Canadian or British port, because of the language. On account of this sailors were prohibited from going ashore at all while the ship was in commission; one can imagine the frustrations of seamen cooped up in their ship and viewing the shore, with all its attractions from green fields to brothels. No doubt many an unthinking hand got himself out of the ship just for a run ashore, and later realized that if he re-joined he would certainly receive a flogging : thus severity built up the offence it was intended to repress.

As a round figure, the total of deaths in the service during the whole period amounted 100,000. The causes of death may be given as percentages of that figure :

Disease	50%
Individual accident, usually when drunk . .	30%
Perils of the sea	13%
Enemy action	7%

Surrounded as we are by antibiotics and vaccines, we scarcely consider the possibility of death by infectious disease, but this practical invulnerability has only arrived since 1950, the long fight beginning with vaccination for smallpox and culminating with the general knowledge of advanced antibiotics. In our war period, the whole of modern medical science was quite unknown, with the exception of vaccination for smallpox, which was quite voluntary and also dangerous owing to the septic tools used. Nobody had dreamt of microbes or viruses; quinine was known and used in fevers; otherwise the usual treatment was to cut a vein and let off some blood, sometimes wiping the fleam which made the incision. Amputations could be quite dextrously performed, and every ship carried a surgeon; but there was only a physician on hospital ships and on each of the first-raters, which usually numbered six. The physicians were paid on an enormously higher rate than the surgeons, somewhere between a captain of a first-rater and a rear-Admiral, whereas the surgeons were paid less than the lieutenants, until the end of the wars – not much more than a pound a week. The consequence was that surgeons fell into two categories: young men who thought it good to have a cruise and see the world between graduating and finding a practice on shore; and those who had failed on shore, usually because of drink, and went to sea to avoid their creditors, pursue their favourable habit free of charge, and if necessary do amputations after an action. Thus, when an epidemic struck on board there was little help from the medical profession.

Scurvy was for long the chief disease in seamen, due to the vitamin deficiency in the diet; but in the wars it affected the Navy very little, as from 1796 a standard ration of lime juice was issued to all hands, and careful captains saw that, where possible, pursers kept a supply of fresh citrus fruit and potatoes, which were not on the ration but available for purchase. Smallpox, which was such a frightful killer on shore, was very seldom found at sea; partly because the air-borne germs cannot carry very far, partly because many had had smallpox and recovered, and partly because vaccination was available free to everybody, (but not compulsory until 1858). Bubonic plague, which is carried by a rat-flea, had ceased to be a menace except in the Mediterranean, where quarantine precautions were taken.

The killer diseases were all insect borne. Typhus, which is carried by a louse, marched with all the armies, who had to be billetted in all sorts of dirty quarters. Of the 25 million men whose lives were sacrified to Napoleon's ambitions, far more were killed by lice than by enemy action. In Britain it was most prevalent in gaols, hospitals and the crowded slums, and once it was conveyed on board ship it was certain that it would spread through all the jammed packs of hammocks. Almost always this disease was picked up when in a British port, and after a ship had been a fortnight at sea without any cases everybody felt better; if it began it was reasonable to assume that a third of the ship's company would die, far more than could happen in the fiercest possible engagement. The senior physicians of the Navy, observing that this fever was associated with dirty conditions (for it was rare in the upper classes), established the regulations already described, whereby every new recruit came aboard in a clean condition. By the end of the wars typhus was far less prevalent in the Navy than in similar classes of people ashore, where the presence of such vermin was regarded as normal. Thus Samuel Pepys, on a journey, 'Up, finding our beds good, but lousy, which made us merry.' 12th June 1668.

By far the greatest killers were the mosquito-borne tropical diseases, malaria and yellow fever. Malaria was not so immediately fatal, and quite frequently death could be averted or at least postponed by quinine, which was well known; but once infected the subject would be liable for the whole of his life to attacks of 'intermittent fever' and a permanent debility. Yellow fever – *vomito negro* the Spaniards expressively called it – was almost always fatal; nobody knew how it was acquired, or how it could be cured; but it was well known that to be ashore on a West Indian island was playing heads-or-tails with death.

In three years service in the West Indies, the British Army lost 40,000 dead by 'Yellow Jack'; at Waterloo, Wellington lost 1,417 British dead; Nelson lost 1,690 dead *and* wounded at Trafalgar.

Individual accident was the next most frequent killer. Sailors were called upon every day to perform feats aloft which would terrify skilled trapeze artists, and there was no safety net. A fall onto the deck was certain death, a fall into the sea probable death. No flotation gear was worn, no lifebelts were carried. The possibility existed that some quick-witted and compassionate officer might throw overboard a hen coop from the quarter-deck, but otherwise there was very little float material about the deck. A ship sailing on a good wind took a lot of stopping; to set the sails aback might carry away a topmast, turning suddenly into the wind might do the same, to wear with it meant going round in a wide circle. The usual way was to heave-to and lower a boat, which would have at least a mile to row before reaching the spot, when it would cruise around for about an hour, depending on the value of the seaman. Sometimes he was found, usually not. Very few seamen could swim, and the art was not encouraged, because it made desertion easier. In northern waters the cold killed very quickly, and in tropical seas there were sharks, although that danger, to *unwounded* men, has been exaggerated. There were many other types of personal accident. There was never full headroom between decks, and caution had to be observed at all times; but a tipsy man is *not* cautious, and there were many deaths by skull fracture from running the head against a beam 'under the influence'. The 'conveniences' for the crew were the 'heads' right forward, consisting merely of unplanked beams at the prow; many a merry sailor who went forward to relieve himself in a seaway pitched over the head, the ship sailed over him, and it might be a long time before he was missed. There were so many hard objects all around, guns and carriages, piles of shot, belaying pins and so on, that any trip or fall could be fatal, especially when drunk, when the instinct to defend the head is dulled.

Perils of the sea in our figures includes explosion, fire (which usually culminated in explosion), foundering and shipwreck. Explosion was very rare although the BOYNE, a splendid three-decker, blew up at her moorings at Spithead, 1st May 1795. The frigate AMPHION blew up alongside the jetty in Plymouth harbour, 22nd September 1796. So far as I am aware, these are all the explosion losses, which compares very favourably with modern times. In 1907 and again in 1911 the French lost a fine battleship by explosion; and during the 1914–18 war, the various combatants lost 13 large vessels by explosion in harbour. Some of the earlier versions of nitroglycerine explosives were found to be very unstable under certain conditions, whereas gunpowder was not affected by the climate.

Accidental fire was was as rare. I am only aware of three cases: the QUEEN CHARLOTTE, 100 guns, off Leghorn, 17th March 1800; the AJAX, 74, off the Dardanelles, 11th February 1807; and the RESISTANCE, 44, in the Banka Straits, 24th July 1798. None of the small warships was lost by such accident, either explosion or fire. It is an error to suppose that a wooden ship is more liable to fire than a steel one; a metal hull can contain plenty of wood and burn out just as completely. In a small ship there were very few places out of observation of anybody, and the first requirement in case of fire is to deal with it immediately.

Foundering was a more serious cause of loss, because the small ships were often out in heavy weather. There was very little foundering among the larger ships (frigates and above) and always it was an old ship which should have been taken out of commission long before; but many of the foundered small ships were quite recent and in good condition. Table III gives a list of all the small ships that foundered, or were supposed to have foundered, during the wars, and the fate of the crew. Studying this, a pattern seems to emerge: there are certain areas of sea which produce more founderings than others.

The table, indeed, lists the areas in which the fiercest storms are expected to be encountered. The very large losses in the West Indies may occasion some surprise nowadays, when the

West Indies are considered a yachtman's paradise, because of course one must always believe the advertisments. But during the hurricane season the West Indian yachtsman puts his vessel into dry dock if he can. At that time there was only a vague idea of a season for hurricanes. Nowadays every hurricane is noted and watched from its birth in the doldrums; the course and speed of the eye of the storm is accurately prognosticated, as well as the force of the winds which swirl round it. At that time there was no idea whatever that a hurricane obeyed any laws at all and could be avoided by prudent navigation; it was the Wrath of God, not an explicable natural phenomenon. It was not until 1830 that Lieutenant Reid of the Royal Engineers read a paper on 'The Law of Storms' to the Royal Society. Near the dead-calm eye of the hurricane, winds up to 200 miles an hour may be encountered, and no small sailing vessel can stand up to them : it must be overwhelmed or capsize, and in such a sea no boat, no man, can live for a minute. The North Atlantic losses were mostly ships sailing to or from Halifax, and it is quite possible that some of them put down as foundered may in fact have run upon icebergs. It was very seldom that there were any survivors to make a report. The North Sea and the English Channel are well known as stormy waters, and many a hurricane which originated in the tropics expends its dying fury round the Island. At Unst in Shetland an anemo-meter reading of 177 m.p.h. was obtained on 15th February 1962. No brig could ride out that. Losses in Eastern waters were very few, because there were very few sloops operating in that area. It was too far for a sloop, until the Cape of Good Hope was taken and made a naval base, and most of the Eastern sloops were Bombay-built.

It is interesting to notice that the number of losses of captured sloops was very little short of losses of British-built ones, although they were not more than a quarter of the sloops in commission; so that the losses of captured sloops was three times the average for British-built sloops. There is no reason to suppose that the foreign-built ships were in any way inferior in design or construction; on the contrary, a ship built in Toulon of Adriatic oak was universally acknowledged to be superior to any British vessel. The possibility exists that if a ship endured a heavy cannonade before surrendering, her timbers would be shaken in a way that might be overlooked in the repair yard, and only show itself in the stress of the storm.

It will be noticed that of the 66 ships lost 48 were lost with all hands, or in 4 cases almost all. This is inevitable in the circumstances: in the midst of the ocean, if the ship itself is overwhelmed by the tempest, what possible hope is there for any man? In shipwreck there is some sort of land somewhere near, and it was quite usual for all or most of the crew to be saved; in action with an enemy there would be casualties, usually light; but foundering was the ultimate catastrophe.

It would be tedious, for me especially, to produce a similar analysis of the 147 wrecks, but we might look at the year of the heaviest losses, 1809. In that year 6 sloops foundered with all hands, three saved in 2 cases. Fifteen were wrecked. One, on the Manacle, lost all hands except a boy; from another, off Martinique, only 19 were saved; in all the other 13 all the crew were saved, except eight in one case and two in another. This may be taken as a typical average, throughout the wars, of the fearsome difference between foundering and shipwreck.

With all those ways of perishing miserably, is it surprising that the sailor looked forward avidly to action with the enemy? Glance again at the little table on page 41; the sailor did not have this in front of him, but he knew the odds well enough. If he were fated to die, even odds he would die in a crowded foetid hospital in the Caribbean, vomiting his guts out in hopeless agony; only three to one against falling off the rigging; eight to one against drowning after a long desperate battle against the elements at their fiercest; and fourteen to one against death in battle. Knowing this, the seaman went merrily into battle, with his mind on prize-money, his eye on the enemy, and his hand on the gun.

3

First Blood

The French government declared war on Britain on 1st February 1793, and immediately ordered the whole navy to be put on a war footing. They impounded all the British merchant shipping in French harbours, more than 70 ships against 8 French merchantmen in British ports. They also urged all the merchants of the sea ports to fit out their fastest ships as privateers and sail forthwith against the returning British ships, which could not yet have heard of the war. The largest of the French privateers were fitted out by the merchants of Bordeaux, but the most nimble were the smaller ones manned by the Bretons, seamen born. A privateer was simply a licensed pirate, who would be treated as a prisoner of war if captured. There was always more of the pirate than the warship about them, discipline was usually lax, and as well as bringing their prizes into French ports they showed great dexterity in robbing their captives of personal possessions.

The brig-sloop SCOURGE was rated as 16 guns, but in time of peace carried only eight 6-pounders, and had not yet mounted her war armament nor complement, for she had only 70 out of her full crew of 90. Under Commander George Brissac she was cruising to the west of the Scilly Islands when she fell in with the French privateer *Sans-Culotte*, with a crew of 81 men, armed with eight long 8-pounders and four 12-pounder carronades, giving her 12 guns and 56 pounds weight of broadside, against the eight guns and 24-pound broadside of the brig. The early privateers were merely the swiftest and strongest of the available merchant ships, with ports cut for their guns, but lacking the stout bulwarks built into the vessel, and the stern discipline built into the crew, of a warship, however small. The the half-armed SCOURGE drew up and engaged; for three hours the fight continued while the ships circled round in the choppy seas, each trying to get a weather advantage of the other. Eventually, after a loss of 9 killed and 20 wounded, the *Sans-Culotte* hauled down her colours and surrendered to a vessel of less than half her gun-power.

This was a most creditable affair for the SCOURGE, whose loss was only 1 man killed and 1 wounded – the very first British blood shed at sea in the wars which were to end more than 22 years later, for this action took place on the 13th March 1793. Nevertheless, there was little notice taken of the engagement, because it was with a privateer, not a French government vessel. Had the *Sans-Culotte* been a regular French naval ship, commanded by a commissioned officer, no doubt there would have been promotions to post rank for the commander and to commander for the lieutenant; but as it was there was nothing but the prize-money, which, as there was no rich cargo, amounted to little. All through the wars this attitude continued, even when the merchants of Bordeaux were sending out privateers as powerful as frigates and commanded by such naval heroes as Captain Bergeret. Given the choice between taking without conflict a few well-laden French merchantmen, yielding lots of prize-money, and engaging a well-armed privateer, with plenty of danger and neither profit or glory to be won, it was only a disciple of Nelson who would go for the privateer. This was an error on the part of Admiralty, which should have treated an engagement with a privateer in exactly the same way as an action with a government ship. Every privateer captured reduced the task of protecting the merchantmen and discouraged *les autres*.

D

It would appear that *Sans-Culotte* was quite a favourite epithet in the first fervour of the Revolution, although I am unaware of any French officer appearing on the quarter-deck in this uniform. One of the very finest ships in the Royalist Navy, the *Dauphin-Royal*, 120 guns, far bigger than anything in the Royal Navy, was re-named *Sans-Culotte* after the Revolution; but Bonaparte, before embarking at Toulon on his expedition to Egypt, renamed her the *Orient*; under which more vice-consular name she blew up at the Battle of the Nile.

The first British Naval officer to lose his life in the wars was Lieutenant John Western. King George III had sent an expedition under the Duke of York to assist the Dutch, who happened to be on the British side at the time. During the amphibious operations which ensued, Lieutenant Western was in command of a shallow-draught gun-boat, and while he was personally aiming a 12-pounder gun he was shot through the head. Casualties were yet few; the Duke of York attended the funeral in Dordrecht Church, and ordered a monument to be erected to his memory. It is to be hoped that the stone-cutters got paid for their labours. However, as the wars increased ceremony lessened, and a warrior did well enough if he were inhumed below wolf level.

A packet-boat, always referred to as a packet, was a small ship, usually cutter or schooner rigged, designed for carrying the mail to any part of the world as well as such passengers as might gain favour with the packet superintendent at a port of call. They were very lightly armed, merely to deal with any fast privateer, and relied on their speed to avoid any more powerful opponent. They were invariably commanded by a steady, elderly, 'plodder' lieutenant, who would carry out his orders without deviation in search of adventure, but was officer enough to fight to the death if necessary in defence of his mails.

HM packet ANTELOPE, Lieutenant Curtis, left Port Royal, Jamaica on 28th November 1793, with mail for England; and three days out, off Cuba, met two French privateers, schooners, apparently well armed and manned. Immediately the ANTELOPE bore up to return to Jamaica, with the two privateers in hot pusuit; one she completely outsailed, but the other kept up all day and all night and all the following day until four o'clock in the afternoon, when the wind fell away to a dead calm. The privateer, which was now made out to be called the *Atalante,* now got out her great sweeps and commenced rowing up to the ANTELOPE, at the same time hoisting the red flag at the main, to inform the attacked that no quarter whatever would be given; always a foolish action, since there is no point in killing an adversary who has ceased to resist, whereas he will fight like a wildcat if surrender also means death.

While the *Atalante* was slowly sweeping herself forward, Lieutenant Curtis had time to consider. He had left Jamaica with a crew of 27, of whom 4 had died of fever, including the second mate; 2 were down with fever, unable to leave their hammocks; so that he had a total of 21 men, far too few to man sweeps, even if he had them. The *Atalante* on the other hand carried 65 men, more than three times his number. For guns, he had six 3-pounders, the smallest gun in the Royal Navy, with a bore of about $2\frac{1}{2}$ inches; whereas the *Atalante* had eight of the same calibre. For responsibility, he had the Royal Mail and also his passengers, some of whom were French Royalists, who might expect short shrift from the Republicans. One of them a former midshipman of the French Royal Navy, volunteered his services, and the other gentlemen assured him that while they were not seamen they could use their swords. Fight it would be, then.

The *Atalante* came alongside at about eight in the afternoon, and the two ships exchanged somewhat scattered broadsides, whereupon the *Atalante,* finding she had to do with an armed ship and a resolute crew, sheered off for the night; but at five the next morning, before first light, she came on again, threw grappling-hooks into the ANTELOPE, fired a broadside, and under cover of the smoke attempted to board. The broadside had the most devastating effect: Lieutenant Curtis was killed, as were also a French passenger and the steward; the first mate was shot through the body and had to leave the deck, although he lived to tell the tale; and the command now devolved on the boatswain, Mr Pasco, supported by the French midshipman aforementioned, M. Nodin, who conducted himself like a hero. He took the helm and worked the ship, and moreover, having a musket and a pike, he defended the stern and quarters against all boarders, shooting them down with his musket, or, if unloaded, leaving the helm to run forward and poke them overboard with his pike. Meanwhile, amidships, Mr Pasco with his minute crew and the passengers repulsed all attempts to board, until the privateer cut the grapples and would have made off; but the bold boatswain ran aloft and lashed the fore-square-sail yard of the schooner to the shrouds of the ANTELOPE. Now a well-directed fire was poured into the deck of the *Atalante*, whose crew now called for quarter, after an action, right alongside, of two hours. Quarter was granted, in spite of the privateer having gone into action with the red (no quarter) flag flying, and next day the ANTELOPE brought her prize into Annotta Bay, Jamaica.

As might be expected in so close and desperate an affray, the casualties were extreme in proportion to the numbers originally engaged. The ANTELOPE out of 21 lost 3 killed, including her commanding officer, and 4 wounded, including her first mate. The *Atalante*'s first and second captains were killed, and 30 men (some accounts say 20, with fair probability) and 17 wounded, out of a total of 65 altogether. Thus one ship lost a third and the other two-thirds of the total complements, as big a casualty list between the two as was ever to be endured again in the whole of the wars. This was an engagement creditable to both parties, but especially to the much smaller British packet-ship, with all the incidents: the French M. Nodin, taking the helm in hand and at the same time guarding the quarter-deck; the French gentlemen repelling boarders with their small-swords; and above all the heroic Boatswain Pasco, taking a command he could never have expected and conducting it with the coolness and initiative of a long-commissioned officer.

There was never a better-fought action during the whole of the 22 years of warfare; but it was merely between a packet and a privateer, and there were neither honours nor rewards for the heroic victors, except of course a bit of prize-money from their capture. It was assumed as a matter of course that any British ship whatsoever could deal with any French privateer, an assumption which was to be very rudely shaken some time later. But however it has been ignored and forgotten, it was a splendid action, bringing out the highest qualities of fighting seamen just as much as at Trafalgar, and *here* at least it will not be forgotten.

4

The Young Viking

Thomas, Lord Cochrane, was one of 'fortune's favourites'. Not only was he son and heir of the ninth Earl of Dundonald, his uncle, Sir Archibald Cochrane, was a distinguished naval officer. His father had served in the Navy, but would rather his son had joined the Army; however, the young man's mind was quite determined on the Navy, and eventually he joined as a midshipman under his uncle, setting foot for the first time on the deck of a warship in June 1793, at the advanced age (for a midshipman) of seventeen years. However, the care of his uncle had put him 'on the books' five years earlier, thus defeating the careful regulations of Samuel Pepys, and enabling him to be appointed acting lieutenant before he was twenty, years before he ever saw a shot fired in anger. Thirsting for service and command, he could never forget that at twenty Nelson was a post captain.

Cochrane was in many ways typical of the Lowland Scottish aristocracy, of Norse origin. Very tall, and even as a young man of a commanding presence, he was well aware of 'the deference due to a man of pedigree'. Where that deference was paid, he was the most affable and charming man imaginable; but he was fiercely resentful of anything resembling a stretch of authority by his seniors in the service. Before action he would gravely consider all the factors; when action was decided on, he was as fierce and headlong as any of his Berserker ancestors, yet always cool and watchful for any circumstance of which he might make use. A 'mariner of infinite resource and sagacity', an ideal commander, but a prickly subordinate.

After service in various ships he found himself, at the end of 1798, a lieutenant on board the BARFLEUR, the flag-ship of Lord Keith (also a Scotsman), Commander-in-Chief of the Mediterranean Fleet. This was the usual position from which 'fortune's favourites' could expect fairly early promotion to commander. Discipline on a flag-ship was always strict, with much formality on the quarter-deck, and First Lieutenant Philip Beaver was the very man to enforce it. He took occasion to reprimand Cochrane in the wardoom, and Cochrane gave offence, not so much by his words but by his disdainful demanour. Beaver immediately demanded a court-martial on Cochrane, which could not be refused. The details are too tedious to recount, and indeed the Admiral found the same. Cochrane was acquitted of whatever he was accused of and advised to respect the position of a first lieutenant, but Beaver was rebuked for his methods; the whole fleet had been delayed a day, when the wind had come fair and they might have been a hundred miles on their way, and this for the most trivial complaint. Beaver, however, was soon promoted post captain, and served with some distinction, dying at the Cape of Good Hope in 1814. Early in 1800 Keith made Cochrane commander in the gun-brig-sloop SPEEDY, and no doubt felt easier for having cleared his quarter-deck of both a martinet and a firebrand.

The SPEEDY was quite small for her class, being 158 tons, with a crew of 6 officers and 84 men; only 2 of the officers were commissioned, Cochrane and his lieutenant, Richard William Parker, the officers otherwise being of warrant rank. The quarters must have been uncommonly tight, for the tonnage only comes to $1\frac{3}{4}$ tons per man, the least I am aware of; a frigate had about 4 tons per man. She could only carry 10 tons of water, about 25 gallons per man, so that she had to re-water every few weeks. The commander's cabin was not big enough for a chair, being entirely occupied by a table surrounded by lockers, forming both storage and seating. The headroom was only five feet, making it difficult for a man of Cochrane's height to get in at all; and when it came to shaving, he had to lift off the skylight, stand up through the opening and set out his tackle on the quarter-deck. Her armament was minute – fourteen long 4-pounders, throwing a shot about the size of a cricket ball. On one occasion Cochrane walked the quarter-deck with a whole broadside – seven shot – of his ship in his coat pockets. Cochrane asked for, and was allowed, two 12-pounder long guns as fore and stern chasers; but there was not room enough to work them, and the timbers would not stand the recoil. Later he asked for 6-pounders instead of his 4s, but the ports were not big enough. The only 'improvement' he was able to make was in his rig : the mainyard requiring to be replaced, a spar was supplied longer than the original; it was ordered to be cut down to size, but instead of doing so Cochrane had the end planed so as to make it appear that it had been cut, and got away with it, so that he could spread in his main course and main-topsail more canvas than the ship was designed for. This may or may not be an improvement. It would appear that Cochrane was under the vulgar delusion that the more sail you hoist the faster you can go. In fact length on the waterline is the limiting factor, and once the optimum sail area for length has been reached, more canvas will by no means increase the speed, but rather decrease it by depressing the bow. The design of sailing ships, indeed of any ship, is a very complicated business, and it is best to accept the ship as it comes from the yard; but then Cochrane always felt that he could do a little better, and history shows that in matters he fully understood this was true.

Cochrane was very proud of his first command. He had not much to survey, but he was monarch as far as it went. This precisely suited him, and he soon endeared himself to his men by his steady but kindly discipline, his care for their comfort, or rather to alleviate their discomforts, and the occasional treat such as fresh vegetables when in port, not only pleasing the men but keeping them healthy and alert. He exercised them at the guns far beyond the Admiralty allowance of powder and shot for practice, and trained them in boarding tactics. Very soon he had a keen and compact company, trained to his hand, eager to do anything he set them at.

The first order was a small convoy job, which was neatly executed, beating off some gun-boats and capturing a French privateer in 1800, bringing the convoy of 14 ships safely into Leghorn. He then rejoined Lord Keith off Genoa, where the French under Massena were occupying the town. Soon, by capitulation, Massena gave up the town and retreated to Nice, and Keith gave Cochrane the orders which exactly suited him — to cruise on the coast of Spain and attack anything in sight. SPEEDY had a wonderful time all June and July, sending seven or eight prizes into Leghorn, where the SPEEDY anchored on Agust 3rd. Lord Keith was highly pleased with the enthusiasm and success of his compatriot, and invited him to share all the festivities which happened to be going on ashore. In a fortnight SPEEDY was at sea again, with orders to harass the coast of Spain but not to risk his vessel against heavy stuff. However, after capturing a small privateer, they fell in with the MUTINE, under a post captain who had a number of French prisoners on board; he ordered Cochrane to take these on board and ship them to Leghorn, which he did rather sulkily, and remained at Leghorn until 14th September, refitting. On the 22nd he captured a large Neapolitan vessel with a French prize crew on board, and brought her into Port Mahon on 5th October. Here he was informed that the depredations of the SPEEDY had attracted the attention of the Spanish authorities, who were fitting out a frigate especially to 'abate the nuisance'. Now the 'infinite resource and sagacity' began to show. There was in the Mediterranean a Danish brig, the *Clomer,* not unlike the SPEEDY: Cochrane painted the SPEEDY in the *Clomer*'s colours, found a Dane somehow and appointed him quartermaster, and found him a Danish naval officer's uniform. The SPEEDY sailed from Port Mahon into the worst winter weather in living memory, and found very little reward. On 21st December a vessel was sighted, which appeared a large and deep-laden merchantman; but as they neared she hoisted Spanish colours and opened her ports to show a formidable battery. SPEEDY hoisted Danish colours, but the Spaniard signalled her to heave-to, and lowered a boat. SPEEDY complied, and also ran up the quarantine flag. When the boat came alongside, the Danish quartermaster explained that this was the *Clomer*, two days out from Algiers, where the plague was known to be raging; but the officer could come on board and see for himself. The invitation was declined, and the ships parted company. The Spaniard was the *Gamo, a* xebec-rigged frigate. Xebec denotes any ship with square sails forward and lateen aft; usually they are quite small coasters, but the *Gamo* was a small frigate of over 600 tons, with two masts square-rigged and a lateen on the mizzen. Her force has been sometimes exaggerated, but in fact she was very much the equivalent of a British sixth-rate 28-gun frigate, mounting twenty-two long 12-pounders on the main deck and eight long 8-pounders and 2 carronades, 24-pounders, on quarter-deck and forecastle, but with a much larger crew than the British equivalent, 319 against 194. Obviously, with a six-to-one superiority, she could eat up the SPEEDY at one mouthful; yet some of the officers of the brig thought they would have liked to have a go at her. Cochrane promised he would think about it, and if it were at all feasible there might be another meeting.

SPEEDY kept on cruising between Cartagena and Barcelona, with great success, coming into Port Mahon on the 24th January with a convoy of prizes. Thence she made for Malta, where Cochrane got himself involved in a silly duel with a French officer of the Royalists, who were there on the Allied side. Fortunately neither was killed, for there were present all the elements of an 'Allied' split. No doubt a Royalist French officer had laid hands upon Cochrane at a fancy dress ball, when he was disguised as a British tar; and to lay hands on a Scottish gentleman is death, naturally: but there were provocations. On the whole, the incident tended to strengthen the establishment view that Cochrane, although a bonny fighter, was a danger to authority, known to be of a Whig family and probably a Radical. This was in fact true, and he remained so all his life; but of course events overtook him and the Radical of 1800 became the staunch establishment of 1860.

Another profitable cruise on the coast of Spain left the SPEEDY with a crew of only 54, due to the prize crews sent with the captured ships to Port Mahon. Off Barcelona a large ship was sighted sailing close under the land, and she was eventually made out to be the *Gamo*. Cochrane piped all hands, told them what was before them, and gave his orders. As the ships approached the *Gamo* fired a gun and hoisted her Spanish colours, the usual way of demanding that a strange ship should identify herself. The SPEEDY hoisted American colours and continued to approach. In the odd sort of sea-etiquette of the period it was perfectly all right to show false colours so long as one hoisted the true colours before opening fire; to fire under false colours laid the whole crew open to the penalties of piracy. The Spaniard hesitated long enough for the SPEEDY to go about on the other tack, when she ran up the British ensign, and the *Gamo* fired a broadside without hitting anything. A second time she fired, also without effect; while the SPEEDY came on in perfect silence, until she ran alongside and locked her yards in the Spaniard's rigging.

This manoeuvre was not bravado: during the previous encounter Cochrane had taken a long look at the *Gamo*, and had noted that not only was her main battery mounted fairly high, her ports did not allow for the guns being depressed. The low-velocity cannon of the period needed a high trajectory to carry any distance; it was a matter of tossing the shot rather than shooting it with velocity. If the port were made large enough to allow of depressing the gun as well as elevating it there would be very little bulwark left to give an impression of protection to the gun-crew. Locked alongside, the SPEEDY was so small and so low in the water that the shot of the *Gamo* roared through her rigging, with damage to the cordage and sails but very little to her men; whereas the little guns of the SPEEDY, being elevated and double-shotted, sent their light shot smashing up through the sides and deck with such effect that the first broadside killed the captain and boatswain. The Spanish next-in-command saw his disadvantage, and gave the order for boarding, which was heard just as clearly on the SPEEDY. When the Spaniards were assembled for boarding, the SPEEDY sheered off, and put a broadside and a volley of musketry into the close ranks. Again and a third time was this manoeuvre repeated, until the Spaniards gave up the idea of boarding and stood to their guns, however little effective.

This, however, could not continue; the SPEEDY was in exactly the position of the lady who went for a ride on a tiger; as long as she remained close enough she could get along well enough, but she could not get away. Cochrane determined to board the *Gamo* with all hands. The surgeon, Mr Guthrie (descended, I believe, from a locally famous Covenanter family), volunteered to take the tiller, and with two or possibly three boys formed the whole ship's complement. With admirable skill he laid the SPEEDY right alongside the *Gamo*, and the boarders leapt up her side, one party at the head and the other at the waist, which was as far as the SPEEDY extended. The boarders at the head had been ordered to blacken their faces and generally make themselves look like pirates, and when they emerged through the gun smoke, yelling like fiends, the Spaniards wavered for a moment; and in that moment they were assailed in flank and rear by the main party. Seeing an opportunity, Cochrane sent a hand to haul down the Spanish colours; the Spaniards supposed that their officers had surrendered the ship, and laid down their arms. It was a legend in the Navy that the surrender was expedited by Cochrane calling to the SPEEDY 'Send another fifty men!' to which the surgeon replied 'Fifty men – aye aye Sir!'

All troubles were not over, for the unwounded prisoners

numbered about 270, almost seven times the unwounded of the SPEEDY. The officers were transferred to the sloop, and the men battened down under hatches; but there must have been very little sleep for Cochrane and his men during the next few days, until they brought their big prize into Port Mahon.

This was perhaps the most astounding single-ship encounter in all recorded history. There have been cases where the weaker ship has defended herself courageously, and sometimes successfully; but never before or since has a ship actually attacked another of an altogether superior class, and conquered. The bare statistics show the amazing disparity of force:

	SPEEDY	*Gamo*
Tonnage	158	Over 600
Main-deck guns	14, 4-pounders	22, 12-pounders
Quarter-deck guns	None	8, 8-pounders, 2 carronades, 24s
Weight of broadside	28 pounds	190 pounds
Total crew	54	319

Of these crews, the SPEEDY lost three killed and nine wounded,* including Lieutenant Parker; the *Gamo* 14 killed, including her captain, and 41 wounded, total 55 casualties, one more than the whole crew with which the SPEEDY went into action.

The news of this astonishing action was rapturously received in England, but Authority was quite cool about it. There was no haste to promote Cochrane post captain, which had rewarded many lesser victors. It may be that Authority felt that the risk was too great and should not have been taken, disregarding the months of thought that had gone into the problem. There may have been jealousy of Cochrane's success, both in glory and in prize-money: in the year's cruise the humblest seaman in the SPEEDY had earned more in prize-money than the regular pay of almost any officer. At any rate, Cochrane's next job

* In his *Autobiography of a Seaman* Cochrane gives the wounded as 18, but he was over 80 years of age at the time, writing 60 years after the event. All other accounts give 9, from the official record, which is also a more usual proportion to the killed.

was to go peaceably to Algiers to expostulate with the Dey about the seizure of a merchant ship, surely a task more suitable for a civilian diplomat, and unsuccessful.

Once more Cochrane was sent to cruise off the coast of Spain, and almost at once captured a Spanish privateer of 8 guns. This he fitted out as a tender to the SPEEDY, and gave the command to his young brother Midshipman the Hon. Archibald Cochrane, who had been with him throughout his service in the ship; a decidedly high-handed proceeding which was unlikely to endear him to Authority. Later they fell in with the KANGAROO, Captain Pulling, and under his orders engaged in a fierce and protracted battle with ships and forts at Oropesa, until they had expended almost all their shot after nine hours' firing, for the SPEEDY could only load 1,400 shot. They now ran in as if to board the ships and attack the fort by land, at which the defenders of the fort 'retired in confusion' and the ships ran themselves ashore; three of them, however, were brought off.

When Cochrane returned with his usual clutch of prizes to Port Mahon he found, to his intense chagrin, that the *Gamo* had not been bought into the service but had been sold very cheaply to the Dey of Algiers. He had confidently hoped that it would have been bought in and that after repair he would command it as a post captain, and again he suspected official jealousy. This may have been an element, but more probably the xebec did not fit at all into the rigging system. Apart from the lateen-rigged mizzen, the sail arrangements on the two square-rigged masts were quite different from anything in British sail lofts. Cochrane's view was that this was all to the good; the lateen rig had proved itself for a thousand years to be the handiest for coasting in the Mediterranean, and the totally un-British appearance was a far better camouflage than a Danish quartermaster.

The next assignment was less rewarding: to convoy a very slow-sailing packet ship with mails to Gibraltar. However, he relieved the tedium by examining all the anchorages along the coast, and came upon a few merchant ships near Alicante. They ran themselves ashore: it would take too long to bring them off, so Cochrane fired them. One of them was laden with oil, and produced a tremendous blaze which, on a very dark night, was visible over a wide area. This attracted the attention of a squadron of three French ships of the line making for the Atlantic, and at five o'clock on the morning of 3rd July 1801 they fell in with the SPEEDY. For four hours they coursed her like greyhounds with a hare, while Cochrane tried every dodge his inventive brain could devise. He had all his guns thrown overboard, and indeed it would have been unwise to have fired them, since the view of the day on the laws of warfare was that it was quite wrong, even criminal, to shoot when there was no possible hope of success. Away went the anchors and the boats, while the SPEEDY tacked and wore and dodged without success; the big French ships were faster and almost as handy, and at length she came under the broadside of the *Desaix*, and the cruise of the SPEEDY was over.

Cochrane never commanded a brig again, because after he was exchanged he eventually got his post rank. His subsequent career as a frigate captain I have related in *The Frigates,* and his later services are part of South American history; but we may have a glimpse of him at the end of his career, when he was the tenth Earl of Dundonald, Admiral and Commander-in-Chief, North American station. From the local newspaper in Bermuda, 21st May 1850:

On Thursday last the noble Earl, the Commander-in-Chief of the Navy, gave a ball, in His Lordship's usual magnificent style, to above 350 persons – comprising the elite of these Islands. . . . The ball was a full dress one; and His Lordship, in full uniform – covered with orders, won in many a desperate encounter – stood to welcome a crowd of guests. Many beheld for the first time this distinguished hero – His Lordship appeared in excellent health and spirits, delighting all with his good humour and urbanity.

5

Heroes Before Agamemnon

There were heroes before Agamemnon, and before Cochrane there were commanders of the little SPEEDY – equally courageous, equally capable, not so brilliant perhaps – and, unlike the predecessors of the King of Men, their names 'stand remembered in the known account of time.'

The SPEEDY has already been described (Chapter 4): a little brig of 158 tons, fourteen 4-pounder guns and about 80 men. In 1798 she was commanded by Hugh Downman and her job was to make a pest of herself on all the coasts of Spain, which was very vulnerable to this kind of attack. The rocky Sierras made a canal system impossible, and as the roads were in rather worse condition than the Romans had left them, practically all traffic had to go by sea.

On 2nd February 1798 the SPEEDY captured a coasting brig, and put into her a prize crew consisting of the sailing master and twelve seamen. The next day, at dawn, about fifty miles west of Vigo, in winds light and variable with a great swell of sea, there appeared a large brig bearing down under all sail on the SPEEDY. This was the *Papillon*, French privateer of 360 tons, four long 12-pounders and ten long 8s with 160 men, making her in tonnage, fire-power and numbers rather more than twice the force of the SPEEDY, which cleared for action. Owing to the lightness of the wind it was 3 p.m. before the

Papillon opened fire at a range of half a mile, while the SPEEDY endeavoured to shorten the range. The cannonade had the usual effect of causing the wind to drop almost to a calm*, and the two ships drifted for more than four hours, firing away in a desultory fashion without much damage to either party, owing to the uncertain heading of the ships and the great swell. At 7.30 p.m. a light evening breeze came up and the *Papillon,* which sailed much better than the SPEEDY, made off out of gunshot, although the SPEEDY got out her sweeps and tried rowing.

At midnight the privateer came upon the brig which the SPEEDY had captured the day before, and fired on her. Mr Marshall, the sailing master, seeing that resistance was out of the question, battened under hatches the twelve Spaniards who were on board, and with his twelve men took to their boat and escaped in the darkness. They had a long twelve-mile pull before they regained the SPEEDY with the bad news. The privateer, instead of handing the brig back to their Spanish allies, put on board a French prize crew of ten men.

At dawn on the 4th the dawn wind enabled the SPEEDY to come up within gunshot of the *Papillon,* which made away until noon, when she put about and made towards the British brig to attack. At 12.30 p.m. a hot and close engagement began, which continued for an hour and a half, when the fire from the *Papillon* perceptibly slackened and the SPEEDY closed in with thoughts of boarding; but the privateer went about and made off right before the wind under all sail. The SPEEDY followed as best she might, but she was the slower ship in any case and was badly cut about in the rigging. As neither ship had a chase-gun they exchanged musket shots for some minutes until the range became too long. Darkness set in, and by 7 p.m. the *Papillon* was completely out of sight.

The SPEEDY now gave up the chase and went right about, beating up slowly against the wind in the hope of falling in with

* See Appendix 1.

E

her prize again. It may have been luck or it may have been seamanship, but at dawn the prize was sighted to windward, and by 10 a.m. the SPEEDY was alongside and re-took her.

The ten French now prisoners had been put on board the prize during the night before the heavy action, and could therefore give no information about the casualties on the *Papillon*, but they were surmised to be heavy, to cause her to run away from a ship of half her force. The SPEEDY lost a lieutenant, boatswain and three seamen killed and four severely wounded, and was so much knocked about, especially in masts and rigging, that she had to put into Lisbon for a complete repair. Her action against a ship so much more powerful was indeed a notable victory, but as the enemy was a privateer and was only beaten off, not captured, little notice was taken of the affair.

When the SPEEDY was recommissioned after repair she was commanded by Jahleel Brenton, based at Gibraltar. On 9th August 1799 she was casually in company with a privateer, the DEFENDER, of Gibraltar, when she sighted and chased three small Spanish warships, having a total of twenty 6-pounders among them. These ran for shelter into a small sandy bay and moored parallel to the shore and very near it, showing an excellent defensive line of broadsides. The shore was so steep-to that no soundings could be found within 200 yards of the Spaniards, so the SPEEDY and the privateer sailed up and down for about two hours, firing away in a desultory sort of way without much effect, Commander Brenton finding out the hard way that it is much easier to hit a moving target than to hit from a moving platform. The privateer, seeing little chance of profit, having only twenty-two of her men on board, and not being under Admiralty orders, made out to sea, informing the SPEEDY that she was going to pick up more men.

The SPEEDY now ran right in, and found anchorage within thirty yards of the middle vessel, opening at once a fierce cannonade. The Spaniards returned it with more good will than skill, until after three-quarters of an hour they lost heart and took to their boats, first cutting the cables of their ships. Two drifted on shore, but the one opposite the SPEEDY was boarded immediately, only two dead men being found on board. The boats were now put out to bring off the two ships which were ashore; quite a hazardous operation, for the Spaniards remained in the thick scrub on the steep shore, keeping up an irregular fire of musketry while the guns of the SPEEDY sprayed the bushes with grape-shot. On such a steep-to shore the ships could not go hard aground; both were got off, and the SPEEDY brought into Gibraltar all three ships, with a total gun-power more than twice her own, and with the loss of no more than two men wounded.

On 3rd October the SPEEDY was passing Gibraltar in heavy weather, wind east, when she saw ten small ships coming out of Algeciras. As a British convoy was in sight Commander Brenton concluded that they were Spanish gun-boats coming out to attack it, and stood towards them. It turned out, however, that they were not gun-boats but eight merchant coasters with two armed vessels, a cutter and a schooner, hoping to slip along the coast unobserved in the dirty weather. When the SPEEDY approached the little convoy scattered, two anchoring under the guns of a fort, while four ran west before the wind pursued by the SPEEDY, and anchored in a bay on the east side of Cape Trafalgar, covered by a fort and an old castle. The SPEEDY was now in the position dreaded by all mariners: embayed with a strong wind driving her onto a lee shore. Commander Brenton anchored half a mile off shore, to give sea-room to work outwards, and opened fire first on the fort and the castle, without any apparent return. With the low-velocity guns of the period the wind made quite a difference, and while the 4-pounders of the SPEEDY could quite well range a mile down wind, the guns of the forts would probably find half a mile too far.

The SPEEDY now turned her guns on the anchored merchantmen, whereupon the crews took to their boats and made ashore, having cut the anchor cables to set the ships adrift.

Commander Brenton now ordered Lieutenant Richard William Parker to take the boats of the brig and either bring off or destroy the ships; a fairly tall order, but the commander knew his lieutenant. The boats were launched and came to the ships, but owing to the heavy surf it was equally impossible to bring them off or to set fire to them. However, they boarded both and brought away all the small arms 'to witness if I lie'; and having satisfied themselves that the ships were complete wrecks, settled down to the long and hazardous pull back to the brig.

Three days later, on 6th November 1799, the SPEEDY was lying-to off Europa Point in a stiff breeze from the west, to escort two ships past the danger area: a brig bound for Trieste and a ship, the UNITY, of great importance, being laden with wine and spirits for the Fleet. Twelve vessels came out from Algeciras, and this time they were all gun-boats carrying 24-pounders: two schooners with two apiece and ten feluccas with one apiece. They could thus bring to bear 336 pounds weight of shot against the 28 pounds of the SPEEDY's broadside. Naturally she made for the gun-boats, opening fire at 3.30 p.m. as they converged on the merchant brig which, under cover of this fire, got clear away and sped through the Straits on the wind. The gun-boats then turned their attention on the UNITY and at 5 p.m. commenced firing on her; but the SPEEDY drove right through the gun-boat flotilla from astern, so close as to carry away quite a number of oars, at the same time cannonading with both broadsides while keeping up a fire of musketry from every man not needed at the guns. What with the rowers sent sprawling as the brig cut through the oars and the rapid fire, the Spaniards fell into confusion and allowed the UNITY to escape; but the SPEEDY kept up the combat, until at 6.30 p.m. the gun-boats desisted and ran for shelter under the guns of Fort Barbary.

The SPEEDY had only two men killed and one wounded, but she was very much damaged in the rigging, and had so many heavy shot below the waterline that she could not make Gibraltar in the strong wind, which would have heeled her enough to let too much water in through the shot-holes, so she ran before the wind for Tetuan Bay, where she did not arrive until 2 a.m. the next morning. Here she anchored to plug her shot-holes, and having made herself more or less seaworthy she stood out and soon came safely into Gibraltar. The Spanish gun-boats remained three days under the guns of the fort and then, instead of returning to Algeciras past the SPEEDY, they went to Malaga where they lay unharmed and harmless for two months.

This desperately unequal combat was fought right under the Rock of Gibraltar, bristling with guns, not one of which was fired in support of the SPEEDY. In explanation the Governor, General O'Hara, informed Commander Brenton, 'I have made arrangements with the Governor of Algeciras, to prevent this town being kept in a constant alarm and annoyance by the Spanish gun-boats, which are in consequence never to be fired on from the Rock.' By all the laws of odds, the SPEEDY should have been either captured or sunk by the gun-boat flotilla, and the governor was quite content to see this happen under the guns of the most powerful fortress in the world, to ensure that nothing should disturb his quiet otiosity!

6

Shipwreck

In 1806–7 Balkan politics were as confused as usual. Since the
French occupation of Egypt, Turkey had been in alliance with
Britain, and also with Russia, quite extraordinarily; there was
a Russian fleet in the Mediterranean. However Turkish diplomatic relations had been resumed with France, and there was a
powerful French army assembling on the east coast of the
Adriatic. The French Ambassador to Constantinople, General
Sebastiani, was using the usual wiles of threats, promises and
bribery to persuade the Turkish government to close the Straits
to the Russians and at least to cool off towards Britain. In
those circumstances the British government had to take account
of possibilities, and Admiralty sent orders to Vice-Admiral Lord
Collingwood, C-in-C Mediterranean, then cruising off Cadiz,
to send a small squadron to reconnoitre the Dardanelles and
the fortifications, in a friendly sort of way, just in case it might
be necessary to be unfriendly later. Lord Collingwood detailed
Rear-Admiral Sir Thomas Louis, in the CANOPUS, 80, with two
74s, a frigate and a sloop. Leaving the Fleet on 2nd November
1806, the squadron arrived at Malta on 8th December, and
on the 21st anchored off the famous island of Tenedos, about
twelve miles south of the entrance to the Dardanelles.

Here they lay for a week, waiting for a favourable wind;
for as there is a constant current running out of the Strait,

which is very narrow, there was no possibility of beating up against a wind off the east. Also they had to collect pilots, who had to be Greeks, for the Turks were not in the least anxious to impart their navigational secrets. Greece was still a province of the vast Turkish empire, but a very restive one: the Greeks looked upon the Turks as their hated oppressors, and on the British as friends whose intervention would some time or other secure their independence; which did indeed happen in 1827.

Having obtained pilots and a good wind, the squadron entered the Strait, and about ten miles inside anchored in a small bay, just short of the heavily fortified narrows. From here, on the 27th December, the CANOPUS proceeded alone to Constantinople, while the other ships made unobtrusive observations from their anchorage. Having transacted his business, with which we have nothing to do here, the Rear-Admiral returned, joining his squadron on 30th January 1807 and immediately sending off the sloop with despatches for Vice-Admiral Lord Collingwood and for England.

The sloop was the NAUTILUS, 18-gun quarter-decked ship-sloop, about 380 tons, with a complement of 122 men. Commander Edward Palmer was an elderly 'plodder' type of commander, perfectly competent in his profession, well liked by his officers and men, unlikely to engage in a brilliant action. Having outlived ambitions of the captains' ladder and flag rank, he looked forward to a quiet retirement on the modest half pay of a retired commander.

The Isles of Greece are much more romantic to enthusiasts like Byron or a travel agent than to those who have to navigate among them in winter. It is difficult enough nowadays, when the waters are charted and buoyed and lighted like Piccadilly Circus, but then it was really hazardous. The islanders, nominally fishermen, were usually more profitably employed as wreckers, smugglers or pirates; charts were not to be completely relied upon; and in winter, in those shallow waters, the fierce squalls kick up a short steep sea almost instantly. The ancient Greeks restricted their voyaging to the summer months, and even then they went ashore every night. However, a sloop of war is not a pleasure yacht, and the NAUTILUS was on duty.

The night came down dark and squally, and the Greek pilot suggested to the commander that they should heave-to and wait for daylight. This was done, and when the pilot could discern his day marks they proceeded through the Archipelago: tricky work; but after the ship had passed between Falconera and Antimilos the pilot turned over to the Commander and went below. Palmer, also feeling tired, pricked out on the chart the proper course for the vessel and also turned into his bunk. It is not precisely known who was left in charge on deck, but presumably the lieutenant and the sailing master. Now the night fell very dark, lightened by almost constant lightning, with an increasing gale from the NE; the NAUTILUS scudded along under double-reefed topsails only at about nine knots. At 2.30 a.m. land was seen abeam; this was taken to be the island of Cerigotto (Andikithera*) and therefore there was nothing but clear sea ahead. The wind and sea increased, far worse than the night before when the ship had hove-to; but the commander was in his bunk and his orders were clear: push on regardless of weather, and anyhow they had passed Cerigotto and all was clear. At 4.30 a.m. the lookout hailed 'Breakers ahead!', and almost immediately the NAUTILUS crashed at full speed upon an uncharted reef.

According to a contemporary account all the men below were thrown out of their hammocks by the shock, but this is impossible: no shock on the hull can throw a man out of a hammock. No doubt they were all startled, leapt up and made a rush for the ladder to the deck, which broke under the strain, leaving most of the men milling about without orders and without object except to get out. There was a period of panic, which the commander and his lieutenant did their best to quell; discipline was to an extent restored, and the officers were able to evaluate the damage. It was clear that the ship must very

* The names given are those in use at the time: the name in parentheses is the modern one.

shortly become a total loss, and the commander and the lieutenant, going below to the commander's cabin, were able to set fire to the despatches and the code of signals. Legalistically, this terminated their responsibilities for their orders, and it would appear that they felt that all other responsibilities had also terminated; there is no further evidence of any kind of chain of command.

Everybody had now more or less got on deck, where the sea was breaking so heavily that they all got into the rigging, in the hope that the ship would hold together and the breaking seas pass beneath. A rock above water was now seen to leeward, and the possibility existed that if the mainmast came down it would fall upon this rock. This did in fact happen about first light, but there was such an undisciplined rush to get over to fairly dry land that several were pushed off into the sea and drowned, one had an arm broken and there were many injuries. Meantime about half-a-dozen sailors took to the whaler and made away without orders. Commander Palmer very properly remained on board until he was sure that every man had left, when he too crossed the shaking spar to the rock.

As daylight advanced the prospect became plainer and grimmer. The reef on which they stood was awash, and while the wreck of the NAUTILUS afforded some protection, it was quickly breaking up and they would shortly be exposed to the full force of the seas. A little distance away was a somewhat higher rock and it was found possible to wade to it, in peril from the many heavy pieces of wreckage which were tossing about all around, some having men clinging to them and hopelessly calling for help where help there was none. The island they finally reached was about 400 by 300 yards and more or less awash except in the centre; here, in the lee of a trifling eminence, they were able to make a fire with a flint, gunpowder and driftwood. It was frightfully cold, the very seawater freezing in the puddles, but the fire, the most primaeval of all comforts, put some heart into the men and they went about collecting driftwood until they had a really satisfying blaze. With odd planks and pieces of sailcloth they put up a bit of a shelter, opposed to the wind and open to the fire, and even got down to taking off their soaked clothing and drying out in front of the luxurious warmth.

At dawn they were cheered by the sight of a small boat approaching the rock; this turned out to be their own whaler, which had been to the uninhabited island of Pera (Pori) where there was no water; so they had made for the light of the fire. There was too much sea for the boat to land, but one of the men invited the commander to make his way through the surf to the boat; this Commander Palmer refused. His place was taken by the Greek pilot, who said there were some fishermen on the nearby island of Cerigotto (Andikithera) who might be induced to help. The boat left, but hope of success was lessened by the renewal of the storm, which drove the waves higher and higher until they extinguished the fire, their comfort and their hope; and drove the men to the highest part of the rock, where they passed a rope round the pinnacle and hung on all night, being constantly dashed against the rocks by the relentless waves until they were all agonisingly cut and bruised, and some, totally exhausted, lost hold of the rope and were swept down into the sea.

Morning broke grey and threatening, although the wind had abated a little; nothing was to be seen except some bodies tossing in the water between the reefs, or thrown upon the rocks. When suddenly, 'Sail ho!' A small ship was seen making directly for the rock. Everybody was signalling frantically with anything they could get. The ship came near, hove-to and lowered a boat: they were saved! The boat approached within fifty yards and was seen to be crewed by men in the dress of European sailors, when suddenly the coxswain waved his hat and the boat at once put about and returned to the ship: Two more boats were lowered and the three parties employed themselves for most of the day collecting the more valuable wreckage from the NAUTILUS, paying no attention whatsoever to the frantic cries and gestures of the famished castaways. As evening approached they all returned to the ship and sailed away with their loot.

It is difficult for us who have been bred under the noble traditions of the Life-Boat Institution and the Humane Society to realise how completely callous people who make a trade of wrecks become. This area had been notorious for thousands of years, ever since Nauplius lit false fires on Point Caphareus to decoy to destruction the Grecian fleet returning from the sack of Troy. But all over the world people who profit from wrecks are noted for their ruthless disregard of the human wreckage – indeed, are just as likely to murder as to save them, so that there may be no witness or claimant. Sir Walter Scott noted a Shetland superstition that if you saved a man from the sea he would be sure to do you a serious injury sooner or later, and has told how on a remote island the natives cut a rope by which eight shipwrecked sailors could have saved themselves, and let them all drown. When Admiral Sir Cloudesley Shovel was wrecked on the Scillies in October 1707 he was washed ashore still alive; an island woman took his emerald ring from his finger and left him to die. Even in 1838, when the steamship KILLARNEY went ashore east of Cork and the survivors made their way to a rock in a little bay, the local peasants paid no attention to them, only to looting; and when the Coastguards eventually rigged a long rope right across the inlet, the peasants came at night, cut the rope and took it away.

The short winter day was succeeded by another long night of suffering, but about midnight they were roused by a hail from the whaler, which returned from Certigotto; amazingly, without a scrap of food, only some water in earthenware jars which could not be got through the surf. The whaler kept off, definitely in fear lest the castaways might seize the boat; but they gave an assurance that the next day they would all be taken off by the fishing boats of Cerigotto, whither the whaler now went. The rest of the night was made even more hideous (it was possible) by the ravings of some of the survivors who had become insane, it was thought from drinking seawater.

On the fourth morning came the sun, the first they had seen since the shipwreck, but it brought little comfort. In all the wide sea it brightened there was no sign of life, no sail, no hope. The day dragged on, and still no hope. They were in the last pangs of starvation, and there on the rocks lay the bodies of their comrades. Was it not better that they should feed on their shipmates rather than the lobsters?

We of this country have supped full of horrors, and the idea of cannibalism does not now arouse the loathing it did a hundred years ago. Its prevalence in certain areas has been attributed to dietary deficiency rather than savage wickedness, and the assertion of the biochemists that all forms of life are essentially identical has had its effect on the moral issue: a steer is as much a fellow creature as a stockbroker. If it is ethical to cut out a dead man's heart in an attempt to prolong another's life, it is certainly ethical to eat it for the same purpose. But regular cannibals had at least their fires and their ovens; here was the uttermost of human misery: the unfortunates huddled separately over the rock, each gnawing fiercely at a lump of raw flesh that had yesterday been a comrade.

That evening the commander and the first lieutenant died, along with a few of the seamen.

Next day there was still nothing to be seen, but some of the men bestirred themselves to make a raft of the wreckage. It was so poorly constructed that when it was pushed out on the sea it came to pieces. Five men now gathered what they could of the remnants and made a very small raft, on which they embarked and were quite swiftly carried away by the current; but they were never seen again.

In the afternoon the whaler again approached, and the men explained the great difficulty they had had in persuading the fishermen of Cerigotto to come out in such unsettled weather, but they had promised to come immediately the weather made a rescue possible. About a dozen of the men attempted to swim out to the whaler: two were taken aboard, which was quite as many as safety permitted, one was drowned, and the rest had to struggle back to the rock as best they could.

The day wore on. One survivor has described his sensations as he watched the sun setting, quite sure that he would never see it again. His sight was failing, unable to focus; he was incapable of connected thought of any kind; his strength was entirely gone, and he lay there quite inert, unable to move a limb, only aware dimly of the sun going down, down for ever. Suddenly there was a shout: the boats had arrived! With a perceptible shock all his lassitude left him: he could see, could think, and arose and made his way through the water to the nearest boat.

At Cerigotto the inhabitants entertained the castaways as well as their very limited means allowed for a fortnight, and then transported them the 25 miles to Cerigo (Kithera), the classic Cythera, where the sea-born Aphrodite came ashore. More important at the moment, there was a British vice-consul. He settled matters with the rescuers and arranged for lodging and medical attention for the rescued, and eventually arranged their passage in a Russian ship to Corfu, then under joint Russo-Turkish occupation, where they arrived on the 2nd March 1807, two months after the shipwreck.

Out of a total complement of 122 men, 58 had been lost. Eighteen were drowned at the time of the wreck, 5 disappeared on the raft, and the other 35 died of starvation on the rock. A sad tale, but it has to be told: life at sea was by no means all one gay adventure.

It would appear that the commander fell short of the qualities expected in a naval officer: amiable, it seems, but weak and easy. In dirty weather and dangerous seas he ought not to have allowed the pilot to leave the deck, but having done so, he should certainly not have turned in himself; there is only one place for the commander in times of danger. After the shipwreck, instead of hoping that the mast would fall right, it could and should have been *made* to fall right; and after it was down, there ought not to have been the panic rush along it to the rock, whereby many were pushed off and drowned. The whaler should not have been allowed to go off on its own. The hull lay most of the night before it broke up, but no attempt was made to organise salvage of food and water. After the commander was dead, *somebody* had enough initiative to make a raft: how much easier the first day while the men were fresh and strong! Hard situations need hard men: Captain Bligh was not an amiable character, but he brought eighteen starving men in a 23-foot open boat for 3,618 miles, without a casualty.

7

Jane's Brother

In March 1800 two British vessels were cruising in the Gulf of Lyons: the 32-gun frigate MERMAID, Captain Robert Dudley Oliver, and the 16-gun brig-sloop PETEREL, Commander Francis William Austen. Captain Oliver ordered Commander Austen to cruise along as close inshore as possible, while he himself would keep company just out of sight of the shore. The PETEREL was to snap up any small prizes available, and if heavier stuff came out was to lure it offshore into seduction reach of the MERMAID: live bait, in short.

On the morning 21st March the PETEREL sighted a convoy of fifty vessels making for Marseille and Toulon, escorted by three armed vessels: a ship, a brig and a xebec. Closing in, the PETEREL cut off and captured two of the merchantmen laden with wheat, put prize crews into them and sent them off. Later in the day the armed vessels came up and brought the PETEREL to action off Cape Couronne. The commodore of this squadron was Captain Raccord, in the xebec *Lejoille,* with six long brass 6-pounders and 50 men; the ship was the *Cerf,* with fourteen long brass 6-pounders and 90 men; and the brig was the *Ligurienne,* with fourteen long brass 6-pounders and two 36-pounder brass carronades, and 104 men. The PETEREL was therefore out-numbered and out-gunned by more than two to one, but engaged the enemy hotly. The MERMAID now came in sight, although at a great distance to leeward, so that it would take hours before she could beat up to take part in the fight; nevertheless the two first-named vessels ran themselves on shore to avoid the action, leaving the brig alone to continue the battle. This she was well able to do, having rather more gun-power and man-power than the PETEREL, plus the aid of a shore battery of four heavy guns. A running fight of an hour and a half ensued until, within six miles of Marseille, the commander of the *Ligurienne*, Lieutenant Pelabond, was killed, and his successor surrendered.

A surprising feature of this duel was the casualty list, after a fight of ninety minutes: the *Ligurienne* had, beside her commander, one other killed and two wounded; while the PETEREL had no casualties whatever, and only trifling damage. Of the ships which ran ashore the *Cerf* became a total loss, but the *Lejoille* was got off and taken in to safety. The *Ligurienne* was a very fine little brig, nearly new and well found in every respect. But her construction was unusual, being fastened with screw-bolts so that she could be taken to pieces and set up as required. The prisoners said that she had been specially constructed in this manner for service with the Egyptian expedition, and there may have been some idea of transporting her over the Isthmus to the Red Sea before it was discovered that the Bombay station had the Red Sea well under control. However that may be, the construction side of Admiralty felt that screw-bolts were likely to work in a seaway, and she was not taken into the Royal Navy.

In August of the same year the PETEREL was in the Eastern Mediterranean in the squadron commanded by Sir Sidney Smith, who was under the orders of Admiral Lord Keith, Commander-in-Chief, Mediterranean. At this time Napoleon, or rather General Bonaparte, had left his army in Egypt and returned to France; his successor, the admired General Kleber, had been assassinated; and *his* successor, General Menou, was by no means admirable. The British strategy was to maintain a strict watch on all the coasts of Egypt; to prevent reinforcements or supplies reaching the French army there; and to prepare for landing a powerful British army to annihilate French authority in Egypt. Egypt was nominally under Turkish suzerainity, and Turkey was in a somewhat wary alliance with Britain, and even with Russia.

The PETEREL, detached on reconnaissance work, was coasting near Alexandria when on 13th August 1800 she sighted a large hull, dismasted and lying on the shoals of Aboukir Bay not far from where the CULLODEN, Captain Troubridge, had stranded while pressing in to join the Battle of the Nile. As the PETEREL approached to investigate, a number of small dhows were seen to leave the ship and make for the shore. At noon the PETEREL anchored in four fathoms and sent a boat aboard the apparently deserted vessel. Very shortly it returned with thirteen Greeks on board, who told the story.

The ship was a Turkish 80-gun line-of-battle ship, which had stranded by night under so much sail that she was dismasted by the shock. In the morning the captain, Indjay Bey, had surrendered to the local French forces, under threat of bombardment from the shore. A considerable part of the crew had escaped in the boats, but the captain and the rest of the crew were taken ashore by the French, except for the Greeks, who had hidden themselves effectively. They did not want to be prisoners of the French, nor did they want to escape to resume their servitude to the Turks; all they wanted was an opportunity to desert. The French intention, the Greeks knew, was to take off all the guns and especially the stores, which they needed badly, and then float off the empty hull if possible.

Commander Austen now sent off his pinnace with the sailing master Mr John Thompson and nine men, with orders to set the ship thoroughly on fire, which was done so effectively that when they left her at 2.30 p.m. the wreck was on fire from stem to stern. The PETEREL waited at anchor until 5 p.m. when, satisfied that the ship was a total loss, she weighed and resumed her patrol.

It was not quite certain how the Turks would regard the

F

burning of a Turkish ship, but Hassan Bey, the commanding officer of the Turkish naval forces co-operating with Sir Sidney Smith, took the correct view that by surrendering it had become a French ship, and signified his approval by presenting Commander Austen with a Damascus sabre and a sable pelisse. Not long after he was made post captain, and thus promoted out of sloop commands. We glimpse him later in command of the CANOPUS, reckoned the finest two-decker afloat (French-built, of course); later still in command of an obsolescent 64-gun ship, the ST ALBANS; not that it mattered as far as promotion went, for that was by seniority only (Chapter 2); all he had to do was to keep on living, and this he did very well, dying at 91. He went up through all the ranks of the Service, was Commander-in-Chief, West Indies, and was awarded the Grand Cross of the Bath. Without doubt, His Excellency Admiral of the Fleet Sir Francis Austen G.C.B. would have been surprised to have been foretold that the only reason for including him in a naval saga was solely because of his half-forgotten sister Jane, who had not married, did a bit of writing, and died at Winchester more than forty years before him.

8

The Viper Has Fangs

A favourite command for a young lieutenant was a cutter – one of those swift little ships which were the errand boys of the Navy. Nowadays Admiralty can communicate instantly with any ship in any part of the world and has been known to take over an operation from the SNC on the spot, with disastrous result; but then the only means was by written orders carried by a ship. Usually this was a cutter: a light single-masted ship of about 100 tons, built for speed and windward qualities, with a crew of about 50; well armed, usually with fourteen 4-pounders in the earlier years, later with ten. With the cutter rig ships could sail closer to the wind than any square-rigged vessel, and were supposed to be able to escape from any larger ship, which did not always happen. The gun-power was enough for a fight, although the crew was rather too small to work the ship and fight her too, which was one of the reasons for reducing the fire-power to ten guns. They were remarkable sea-boats, and could sail anywhere in the world.

On 13th March 1797 the 14-gun cutter VIPER, Lieutenant John Pengelly, having done an errand to Algiers was returning to Gibraltar. Passing north of the little island of Alboran she sighted a sail and went NW in chase. This sighting was a Spanish privateer brig, much the same force as the VIPER, having six 4-pounders, four 6-pounders and eight swivels, with 42 men.

The cutter overtook the brig in half an hour and commenced firing, gradually closing the range until the Spaniard tried to stave her off by throwing on her deck flasks filled with gunpowder and sulphur, which the crew got rid of overboard without much trouble. When the privateer saw that the VIPER was preparing to board, she hauled down her colours and surrendered. She had a fair amount of damage, with two killed and six wounded. The VIPER had about 40 shot in her hull and one through her mast, but had no casualties whatever, so that there was nothing to dim the pride with which she brought her prize into Gibraltar.

On the 26th December 1799 the VIPER, still commanded by Lieutenant Pengelly, was off the coast of his native Cornwall not far from Falmouth when she sighted a suspicious sail and went to investigate. Soon there was seen the unmistakable rig of a French *chasse-marée*, which was in fact the privateer *Furet*, Captain Bouvet, armed exactly as the VIPER with fourteen 4-pounders. She had actually picked up a prize that very morning and sent her to France with a prize crew, leaving the *Furet* with 57 men. These privateers were a continual plague in the Channel: fast and seaworthy, manned by the intrepid and expert mariners of Britanny, they could nip out of port in almost any weather, pick up a prize or two, and be back among their rocks and races before any warship even heard of them. Even if they did meet an armed ship, speed and skill would generally bring them clear away. On this occasion the *Furet* saw nothing about the cutter to cause alarm, and waited to engage; but after a cannonade of about three-quarters of an hour decided that this was not a good idea and made off. The VIPER was just as handy and as well manned and engaged her in a running fight for an hour and a half, until damage to the *Furet*'s rigging allowed the VIPER to come alongside, when two broadsides were decisive and the privateer surrendered. She was extensively damaged and had lost four killed and eight wounded, including her captain and second captain. The VIPER had only two slightly wounded (one, Lieutenant Pengelly) and had to have a new mast after she brought her prize into Plymouth; with some triumph, for these odd-looking luggers were hard to catch and hard to beat.

December in the Channel, July in the West Indies – never a dull moment for a cutter. Now she was attached to a squadron under the command of Sir Edward Pellew, lying off Fort de France, Martinique and commanded by Acting Lieutenant Jeremiah Coghlan. Jeremiah was a rarity among 'fortune's favourites'. A poor boy, he had entered the merchant service as a ship's boy in 1793; three years later he distinguished himself for courage and resource in the rescue of the crew of a wrecked East Indiaman. The account came to the notice of Sir Edward Pellew, then in command of the INDEFATIGABLE, and he forthwith wrote to the young hero, offering him his patronage if he cared to join the Royal Navy. Imagine the feelings of a poor ship's boy on receiving such a letter from so distinguished a captain! He accepted, joined the INDEFATIGABLE and was immediately rated midshipman, quite correctly, for he had the requisite sea experience. Pellew never regretted his offer, and when he moved to the IMPETEUX, 74, in command of a squadron, he took Jeremiah with him. Now, with most of his required five years as a midshipman behind him and in command of a fine cutter as acting lieutenant, Jeremiah burned to justify Sir Edward's patronage.

Fort de France was the principal French naval base in the West Indies, and was appropriately guarded. A line-of-battle ship and two frigates were in the harbour; the narrow entrance was covered by three batteries of heavy guns and gun-brigs and smaller gun-boats on constant watch and patrol. Altogether the coast defences mounted more than 250 guns. It was impossible to contemplate a serious attack on such a fortress, and indeed it was not taken until 1809, and then by a fleet of 28 warships of all sizes and an army of 10,000 men. Still, Coghlan felt that the VIPER should have a bite somehow, and exercised his brains on all sorts of unlikely schemes.

The outermost of the gun-brigs was the *Cerbère*, and

Jeremiah studied her with the loving care of a hunter. She was moored broadside on to the channel, close under the batteries, and mounted three long 24-pounders and four 6-pounders, with 87 men. At length Coghlan thought of something and went to Sir Edward, who gave him permission to try. He asked from the flag-ship the 10-oared cutter and twelve volunteers, in which he was to go himself along with Midshipman Paddon from the VIPER and six of her men; there was also another boat from the VIPER and a third from the frigate AMETHYST. On the very dark night of 26th July 1800 the little flotilla set out.

The general idea in a cutting-out-by-boats action was to have a number of boats boarding the attacked vessel at different points, to confuse the defenders who could not tell when yet another boatload might come aboard. In this case such tactics did not work, for the two smaller boats could not keep up with the 10-oared cutter and lost all touch in the darkness, so that the cutter was alone when she reached the *Cerbère,* which was fully alerted to the attack. Undaunted, Coghlan attacked on the quarter, leapt over the bulwark and fell into the meshes of a trawl-net which had been hung up to dry. Thus entangled, he was wounded in the thigh by a thrust from a boarding pike, and he and his handful of men were all bundled overboard. They now pulled forward and boarded again on the forecastle, were able to establish themselves and commenced a fierce fight with the defenders; but once again they were defeated and forced overboard. Undiscouraged, they returned to the attack with renewed ferocity, and this time, after a desperate struggle, they actually carried the ship. The other two boats arrived in time to help tow the brig out, which they did under a heavy fire from the batteries, which scored no hits.

Out of 87 defenders, there were 6 killed and 20 wounded; the 22 who conquered them had 1 man killed and 8 wounded, including Coghlan in two places and Paddon in six.

This was a splendid affair: it is difficult to get men to charge a second time after a repulse; to charge and win on a third attempt is very rare indeed and tells better than words the quality of the score of volunteers and their young leaders. The action was fully appreciated by those who were best able to judge. The prize-money for the *Cerbère* belonged to the whole squadron, but the officers and men unanimously decided that it should all go to the boat's crew which had done the job. In his report to the First Lord, Earl St Vincent, Pellew refers to 'my admiration of that courage which, hand to hand, gave victory to a handful of brave fellows over four times their number, and of that skill which formed, conducted and effected so daring an enterprise.' St Vincent went out of his way to encourage so promising an officer: he sent him a fine sword, and even strained the rules – very rare for him – to confirm his commission as lieutenant six months before he had served the necessary five years as midshipman.

This was a very fair start, and by 1805 Jeremiah Coghlan was commander of the 18-gun ship-sloop RENARD, cruising in the West Indies. On 20th March 1805 off the north coast of Dominica a sail was sighted and chased, on which the stranger, nothing loath, shortened sail to engage. This was a 20-gun privateer sloop, which had had a rather chequered career. Originally a Bermuda trader, she was bought into the Royal Navy in 1795, armed, and renamed the LILY. In 1804 she was captured by a French privateer, taken into Guadeloupe and fitted out as a privateer under the name of *General-Ernouf*, after the governor of the island. Like the RENARD, she had two long 6-pounders, but while she had two more carronades, hers were all old pattern British 12-pounders, very short and of little power, while the RENARD's were 18-pounders of an improved type; and although the French ship had a larger crew, Coghlan had trained his men into a fine team, keen and taut, as might be expected of him.

The *General-Ernouf* began the action, firing irregularly at a range far too long to be effective. The RENARD waited until she was alongside her opponent, at about 40 yards, when she gave her a simultaneous broadside of devastating effect, every shot crashing into her hull, followed by a rapid succession of broadsides equally well controlled and equally accurate, such as the privateersmen had never dreamt of. After half an hour the *General-Ernouf* was seen to be on fire, and ten minutes later she blew up in a great explosion. The RENARD had only one boat left undamaged by shot; this was immediately launched, and the RENARD sailed slowly around towing pieces of timber through the water. By these means 55 men were rescued, the remaining 105 of the French crew being lost. The RENARD had no casualties whatever, showing how effective a defence is a rapid and accurate fire on the enemy.

Although it was common practice to set fire to a captured vessel which was not worth bringing away, it was very seldom indeed that one took fire and blew up during an engagement. The case of the *Orient* at Aboukir springs immediately to the mind, but the sensation which this caused shows how rare it was at the period – strangely enough, considering the amount of gunpowder, slow-match and other combustibles always about during battle.

Jeremiah Coghlan must have reflected, as he was writing in his cabin that afternoon, that just ten years before he had been a merchant ship's boy, the lowest form of marine life, everybody's kickabout; and here he was in command of a fine warship, writing his official letter to the Commander-in-Chief to report a very complete victory with no losses on his ship. He had further to go, because it was not long before he became a post captain, although he never achieved flag rank. It was too late in the war, and there were nearly 700 on the captains' ladder in front of him; still, it was the highest rank to which one could be *promoted*. Jeremiah Coghlan is a standing proof that whatever has been said, and truly said, about influence and connections, it was still possible for a youth in the humblest civilian rank, without money or influence of any kind, to reach high Naval command by sheer merit. How would he fare today?

9

The Hirelings

In addition to the potential of the Royal and private dockyards, there was another source of ships for the Royal Navy – merchant ships already in service, which could be either bought or hired. The larger ships such as the East Indiamen were usually bought, for the alterations they required and the service they might have to undertake would make it difficult to return them; but very often the smaller ships were hired. Quite frequently there was a need for small ships with a special rig which did not come within Admiralty specifications but suited a particular area at the time, and there was a perennial shortage of small swift vessels for carrying despatches and important passengers. The usual practice was that Admiralty hired a vessel complete with her crew, paying the owners so much per month, sometimes for a definite period and sometimes indefinitely, and put a commissioned officer in command, the former skipper generally remaining as sailing master. Out of the hire the owners paid the skipper and crew, and kept the ship seaworthy; but war damage fell on Admiralty. This suited all round: Admiralty had immediate use of a ship and crew; the men were fed and paid as they usually were plus having a chance of prize-money, although they were outside the Navy scheme for pensions for wounds; and for the owners, while it was not so potentially profitable as fitting out a privateer, at least there was a sure income and no financial risk.

On 28th September 1795 the hired cutter ROSE, Lieutenant William Walker, was on a passage from the fleet at Leghorn to Bastia in Corsica. She was armed with eight 4-pounders, but carried a crew of only thirteen men and one boy, conforming to merchant rather than Navy standards, which would have given her forty or fifty; even a 4-pounder gun weighs almost half a ton, and was in the Navy handled by four men, and there must be enough others to work the ship and replace casualties. Of course, only one broadside was manned as a usual thing, although the possibility always existed of a ship being engaged on both sides. The little cutter, with her miniscule crew, had on board a King's Messenger, doubtless with important despatches, two ladies, and £10,000 in coin.

At 4.30 in the morning the only man on deck, the steersman at the tiller, saw three suspicious ships to leeward and called the lieutenant. The ships were recognised as French privateer feluccas, which were known to be well armed and to carry crews of from forty to sixty men; they were also very fast and handy. Lieutenant Walker decided that he could best defend his weighty responsibilities by attacking, called his men, cleared for action and made for the nearest felucca. Intending close action or boarding, he had each gun loaded with three shot, which one could do safely enough with 4-pounders, tough little pop-guns.

Lieutenant Walker intended to run his opponent on board amidships and attack with the cutlass. With this in view he took the tiller himself, but as they neared he went forward to lead the boarders. The steersman did not quite carry out his orders, but with the bowsprit carried away the felucca's mizzen mast and swung under her stern; really a far better manoeuvre, for she was now able to give a most effective raking broadside. Coming round on the lee side, she was almost becalmed by the huge lateen sails of the felucca, but was able to fire her other broadside, on which the privateer hauled down her colours and her captain called for quarter. Lieutenant Walker had not a man to spare to put on board, so he ordered the captain to brail up his sails and lie-to, threatening to sink her with all hands if she attempted to escape, while he made after the next privateer. Coming close alongside, a single broadside of his treble-shotted 4-pounders, aimed low, actually sank her. Leaving the crew to sink or swim as they preferred, Walker went after the third, which, however, made off to windward. No British-built ship could outsail a felucca on that tack, so abandoning the pursuit he returned to his first capture, which still had twice as many men alive as his whole crew. It was impossible to spare a prize crew, so Walker battened the whole crew down under hatches, put on one sentry and a steersman, and took the ship in tow, bringing her in triumph into Bastia.

The first privateer had originally a crew of 42 men, of whom 13 were killed and an unstated number wounded; they reported the other two feluccas as manned with 56 (all lost) and 48 (all escaped), so that the little ROSE had taken on, in men, ten times her number. The captured felucca was armed rather as a pirate, well fitted for taking merchantmen : she had one long brass 6-pounder and four 1-pound swivels forward, while on her gunwales she mounted twelve wall-musketoons. The ROSE had only one man wounded, and that by the accident of a gun-carriage running over his foot on the recoil, crushing it badly; a painful and crippling wound, but William Brown declined to leave the deck, saying he could use a musket sitting as well as anybody. The ship, however, was extensively damaged.

This splendid little action was quickly known around the Mediterranean, and Walker received the congratulations both of Sir Gilbert Elliot, Governor of Corsica, and of Admiral Hotham, C-in-C at Leghorn; but as the ROSE was not a King's Ship, and the action was with privateers, it was not reported in the *Gazette* and Walker had no promotion nor recognition of any kind.

The hired cutter COURIER, twelve 4-pounders and 40 men, Lieutenant Thomas Searle, was on her way from Yarmouth to the Texel, where an amphibious operation was mounting. On 12th May 1799 she came across an enemy brig just in the act of capturing a British merchant sloop. The brig was a privateer of 16 guns, probably 6-pounders, and the action continued for almost two hours, when the brig made off; the COURIER chased her until midnight but lost her in the mists. Next morning a two-masted ship was descried, but on closer approach it turned out to be a small schooner, the French privateer *Ribotteur,* with four 3-pounder guns and 26 men, which surrendered without resistance; she had been a consort of the brig chased the day before. The loss of the COURIER in the two little engagements was five men wounded.

On 11th August 1799 the COURIER was part of a light squadron mudlarking in the shallow narrow passes between the Dutch islands. One objective was to retake the brig *Crash,* which had been captured by the Dutch and now lay moored in a narrow strait off Groningen. She was armed with twelve heavy carronades, 18, 24, and 32-pounders, and was well situated and difficult of access, the wind blowing dead against the attackers in a very narrow and shallow passage. The main force was two sloops, which had great difficulty in tacking among so much mud and so little water. The COURIER with her cutter rig could sail much nearer the wind, so Lieutenant Searle was sent ahead to engage the *Crash* and prevent her escaping before the sloops could come up. This he did with effect, although within very close range of the big carronades of the brig. To engage 32-pounders with 4-pounders seems a tall order, but the COURIER in fact sustained no casualties, although naturally some damage. Eventually the sloops came up and the brig surrendered.

The CRASH was repaired overnight and along with the COURIER sent inshore to cover a boat operation against a battery on shore. In the shallows and rushing tides both grounded and were got off with difficulty, having taken no part in the action which, however, was completely successful, the boating party carrying the battery, spiking the heavy guns and taking away two brass light 4-pounders as souvenirs.

On the evening of the 22nd November 1799, while the COURIER was cruising off Flushing, a cutter was observed to bring-to a bark, and the COURIER went to investigate, upon which the cutter made off. The bark was a British merchantman, and informed the COURIER that she had been held up by a French privateer. Lieutenant Searle at once chased northwards all night, and at 9 a.m. overtook about thirty miles east of Lowestoft. The privateer was well armed with fourteen 4-pounders and 44 men, Captain Lallemand, and the action lasted an hour, when the French ship surrendered. She lost four killed and six wounded, while the COURIER had one killed (her sailing master) and two wounded.

All this small stuff was good service, and satisfied Admiralty that Lieutenant Searle was of captain quality; he was promoted commander and eventually captain, a considerable encouragement to other lieutenants in command of hired vessels, which was generally considered the lowest form of commissioned-officer life.

Another fortunate lieutenant was William Wooldridge, in command of the hired brig PASLEY, with fourteen old-type 12-pounder carronades and two long 6s, and 54 men and boys. On 21st July 1801 she was about thirty miles south of Majorca in light irregular winds when she came up with a large Spanish xebec of 22 guns, which demanded her surrender. The natural reply was a broadside, and the action continued for more than an hour. The wind died away completely because of the cannonade (see Appendix 1), and the xebec, having had enough of this rough stuff, got out her sweeps and rowed away. The PASLEY also swept after her, but having a much smaller crew could not keep up, and the xebec got safely to Ibiza and took shelter under the shore batteries. Her name and losses are not known to me; the PASLEY had one killed and two wounded.

On the 28th October 1801, about seventy miles SE of Cartagena, the PASLEY fell in with a three-masted Spanish privateer polacre, the *Virgen-del-Rosario*, with eight long 12-pounders and two long 24s, and 94 men. Coming up from windward, she chased the PASLEY, came alongside, and there commenced a furious cannonade which lasted for an hour. The PASLEY'S weak old carronades (pages 16, 87) were no match for the heavy long guns of the Spaniard, so moving ahead she crossed the bows of her opponent, caught her bowsprit, lashed it to her capstan, and instantly boarded. There ensued a most desperate hand-to-hand battle on the deck, but after fifteen furious minutes the *Virgen-del-Rosario* was completely conquered. As usual in a boarding action, the losses were very heavy – kill or be killed.

The PASLEY had three killed, including the gunner, her sailing master mortally wounded, and seven wounded, including Lieutenant Wooldridge and the mate. The privateer had 21 killed, including almost all her officers, and 13 wounded.

It is difficult to praise in words the cold courage of Lieutenant Wooldridge: finding himself quite out-gunned by his powerful opponent, he boarded a ship which had almost twice his man-power, and carried her with the cutlass. Admiralty approved, and made him commander and then captain; in command of the frigate MEDIATOR on 11th April 1809 he led in the fireships for the attack on the French fleet in Aix Roads (*The Frigates,* pages 112–3).

Lieutenant Thomas Henry Wilson commanded the hired cutter LARK, with twelve old-type 12-pounder carronades and two long 4-pounders, and a crew of 50 men and boys. Cruising off the Texel, he fell in with, and engaged, a French privateer, which ran herself ashore. In the tides and shoals the LARK was unable to get close enough for effective action, and had to give over; on the night tide the privateer was able to get off and away.

A few days later, on the 25th April 1800, the LARK came up with a well-known French cutter privateer which had been having a fine time capturing British merchantmen in the narrow seas: the *Imprenable,* with twelve long 3-pounders and two long 8s, 60 men. After a sharp engagement with the LARK she too ran herself on shore, from which unsinkable position she fought for another hour, when her men began to escape to the land to join a party of soldiers numbering perhaps a hundred. Here they took up a position among the dunes, to oppose with musketry any attempt to bring off their ship. Lieutenant Wilson, however, was getting a little peeved with this running-ashore tactic. He had only two boats. He ordered the sailing master to take the larger with as many men as she would hold, and land a little distance away, to take in the flank the musketeers among the dunes, while he himself in the small boat boarded the cutter. Everything happened according to plan (O Rarity!) and Lieutenant Wilson brought his prize into Yarmouth Roads without a single casualty.

Success is gratifying, but there are occasions where doing one's duty to the last is the only gratification. On 3rd April 1804 the hired cutter SWIFT, 77 tons, eight 4-pounders, 23 men and boys, Lieutenant Leake, bearing despatches to Vice-Admiral Lord Nelson off Toulon, was overtaken by a French xebec privateer of double her size, gun-power and crew. Seeing the probable outcome of the impending battle, the despatches were weighted and hove overboard, and in the furious engagement which ensued the lieutenant and many of his men were killed and the cutter captured. As has been said, these small errand-ships depended on their speed to keep out of trouble, and it was bad luck to fall in with a xebec, which is even faster under Mediterranean conditions; but Lieutenant Leake did his duty to the last.

In 1808, by one of those changes of political wind which we need not here examine, Britain was in alliance with Sweden in opposition to Denmark and Russia. Vice-Admiral Sir James Saumarez, wearing his flag in the VICTORY, commanded a strong fleet in the Sound, and had detached Rear-Admiral Sir Samuel Hood with the 74s CENTAUR and IMPLACABLE to cooperate with the Swedish fleet. Having occasion to communicate with the Rear-Admiral, Saumarez sent his despatches by the hired cutter SWAN, Lieutenant Mark Lucas, with ten 12-pounder carronades and 40 men.

On 24th May 1808, off the island of Bornholm, a strange cutter was seen making out from the land towards the SWAN; this seemed to be much the same sort of ship, perhaps larger, and well manned. After the usual manoeuvring for the wind, false colours, and so on, the two ships engaged at about 4 p.m. about a mile from a battery on Bornholm, which opened fire without any effect at that range. The enemy had apparently a fairly large long gun mounted in her stern, and in endeavouring to bring this to bear she hung in stays. While she was thus immobile the SWAN was able to get in several broadsides, and shortly she blew up with a massive explosion. The cannonade and explosion had practically killed what wind there was; the battery on Bornholm was firing with more rapidity, and boats were pulling out from the shore. Lieutenant Lucas did not wait to seek for possible survivors, and therefore the Danish cutter was not identified. In his official letter Vice-Admiral Saumarez gave high praise to Lieutenant Lucas for his spirited action, although another Commander-in-Chief might have felt that it was more important to deliver his despatches than to trail the coat; but Saumarez was the last man in the world to discourage a fighter.

1 A French chasse-marée chased by a brig

2 The SCOURGE and the *Sans-Culotte*

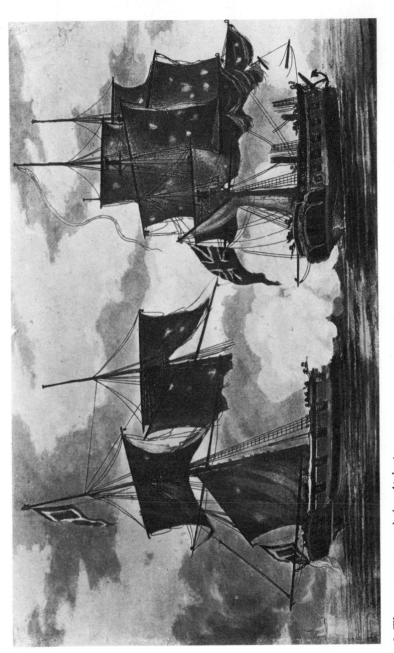

3 The ANTELOPE and the *Atalante*

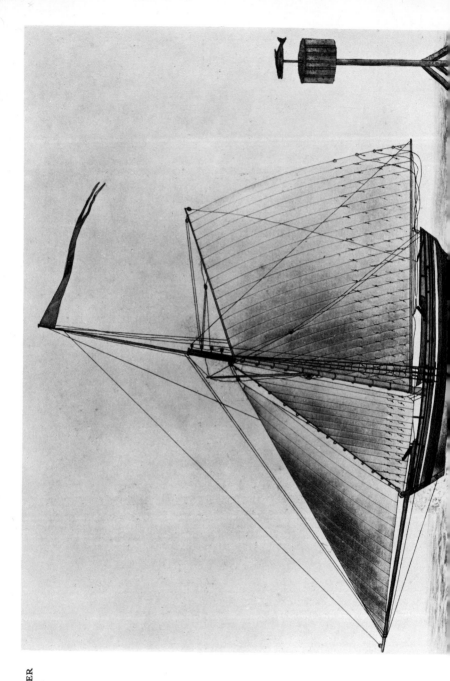

4 The VIPER

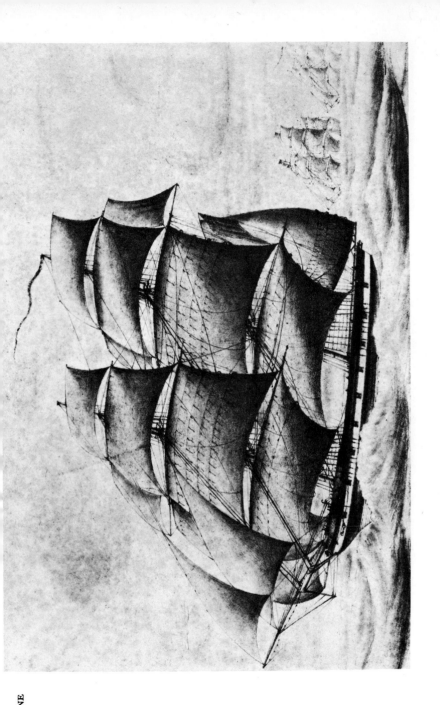

5 The
WOLVERINE

7 James Cook

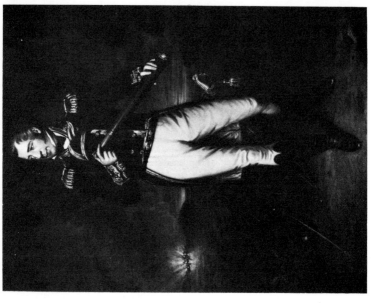

6 Thomas, Lord Cochrane

8 The *Wasp* and the REINDEER

9 The *Hornet* sinking the PEACOCK

10

The Mails Must Get Through

Packet-ships have already been described (Chapter 3), as well
as the splendid action of the ANTELOPE with the French
privateer *Atalante*. In fact, when a packet *was* engaged it was
usually with a privateer, because these were the only enemy
ships fast enough to catch up with packets, which were
generally fast cutters able to sail very close to the wind and
designed to evade any enemy ship of war. Privateers had also
to be fast, to overtake merchantmen and get away from warships; moreover they carried very large crews for their size,
for boarding, providing prize crews, and manning the long
sweeps they used extensively in calms.

In the Royal Navy then as now it has been usual to give
some idea of the ship by its name; thus one could be fairly
sure that the ROYAL SOVEREIGN would be a ship of the
line, the AMAZON a frigate, and the CURLEW a brig. Not so with
the mail packets, which were frequently given very high-
sounding names, seemingly fitter for three-deckers than for tiny
cutters. Thus the PRINCESS ROYAL was in fact a cutter of 6 guns,
four 4-pounders and two 6s, and a crew of 32 men and boys,
commanded by Lieutenant John Skinner as a nice light job
for a semi-cripple, for he had lost his right arm in a frigate
engagement in the War of the American Revolution. On
12th June 1798 the PRINCESS ROYAL left Falmouth for New

G.

York, carrying the mails and seventeen passengers, including the commander's sister and her maid.

On the 21st June, at dawn, there appeared a large brig, which made all sail in pursuit. This was the Bordeaux privateer *Aventurier,* of 16 guns, fourteen long 4-pounders and two carronades, 12-pounders, with a crew of 85 men and boys, nearly three times the force of the packet, which very properly set all sail to escape. The privateer now got out her sweeps, as there was practically no wind and the sea very smooth, and after fourteen hours' rowing came within shot of the PRINCESS ROYAL, when both ships fired to try the range. Apparently satisfied that she could take the packet without trouble, and being disinclined to risk a night engagement, the *Aventurier* took in her sweeps and lay astern of the PRINCESS ROYAL.

Dawn comes early at midsummer, and at 3.30 a.m. the *Aventurier* appeared alongside within pistol-shot, and opened fire. All the passengers had volunteered their services, making a very useful addition to the minute crew of the PRINCESS ROYAL. The most valuable was a Navy lieutenant who was on his way out to join his ship, the ST ALBANS, 64; he took charge of the after 6-pounder and showed himself to be a highly skilled gun-layer. The other fourteen gentlemen were issued with a musket apiece, and were as cool as ever they were over spaniels, while Miss Skinner and her maid were employed below, sewing and filling bag-cartridges for the 4-pounders. The guns were hove about so that five of the six could bear on the broadside, and they were served as steadily as if there were no such things as musket-bullets and cannon balls whistling and crashing around. They fired broadsides only, taking their time from the ST ALBANS lieutenant, and while they were reloading the sporting musketeers made the enemy keep their heads down.

For two hours this cannonade of sixteen guns continued against six, when the *Aventurier* decided to call it a day, got out her sweeps and rowed off eastward. Immediately the lieutenant's 6-pounder was hove around to bear as a stern-chaser, and before the privateer was out of range he got off two shots, both of which crashed through the stern of the *Aventurier* to the cheers of the crew of the PRINCESS ROYAL, who then went to breakfast before seeing to the repairs. These were not too difficult : several shot in the hull, all above water; the boats and spare spars knocked about, and the sails and rigging cut; but the masts and spars undamaged and, strangest of all, not a single casualty.

The *Aventurier*, on the other hand, had two killed and four wounded, all her masts shot through and nineteen shot in her hull; so badly knocked about, in fact, that she had to give up the adventure and go back to Bordeaux to be completely re-fitted. There she landed thirty civilian prisoners, British and American, taken from former prizes during that cruise, and from these all the details of the *Aventurier*'s losses were ascertained.

As always when the battle was against a privateer, however well equipped, there was no particular recognition of this splendid little action. There was no prize to show, only the story of a privateer beaten off; but a story fully authenticated, proving that an elderly and one-armed packet commander was still a King's Officer, completely capable of a heroic and successful action against enormous odds.

The WINDSOR CASTLE was not a three-decker flag-ship but the Leeward Islands packet, Acting Commander William Rogers, six long 4-pounders and two 9-pounder carronades, with a crew of 28 men and boys. The carronades were unusally small, the smallest normal carronade being a 12-pounder, but 9s were probably as heavy as the WINDSOR CASTLE could mount. On 1st October 1807 she was making for Barbados with no passengers but very heavy mails when she sighted a large top-sail schooner approaching under a press of sail. This was the privateer *Jeune-Richard,* having six long 6-pounders and a single long 18-pounder on a traversing carriage, so as to be worked on either side; her complement was 92 men. Not wishing to speak her, the packet cracked on all sail to get away; but the schooner was much the faster ship and came up hand over fist, hoisting French colours and opening fire, which was returned.

Coming within hail, the privateer demanded the surrender of the packet, which was refused. The schooner now came close alongside, threw in grappling-hooks and tried to board; but Commander Rogers had issued pikes to his crew, which they used so effectively as to repulse the boarders with considerable loss. The French now cut the ropes of the grappling-hooks with the intention of giving up the attempt, but the yard of the topsail was so entangled in the packet's rigging that the ships remained locked together. Both sides now prepared for a second hand-to-hand combat. Preparing for the worst, Commander Rogers had all the mailbags hung out overside on the disengaged side, and stationed two boys with hatchets to cut the ropes and let the mail go if the enemy should appear to get the upper hand.

The privateer's men now gathered together on deck with the intention of making a concerted rush; but Commander Rogers had prepared one of his 9-pounder carronades, loaded to the muzzle with grape-shot and musket-balls, and this was now fired with fearsome effect into the crowd on the opposite deck. Without giving the enemy a second to recover from the blow, Commander Rogers leapt upon her deck, followed by five of his men, all that could be spared of the survivors. This tiny body of determined men fell upon their confused and frightened opponents, and in spite of apparently overwhelming numbers drove them all below with heavy loss and fastened the hatches on them : then down came the French colours.

The casualties in this desperate engagement were extremely heavy, as almost always in a boarding action, when it is kill or be killed. Out of a total of 28, the WINDSOR CASTLE lost 3 killed and 10 wounded. Out of 92, the *Jeune-Richard* lost 21 killed and 33 wounded, much more than half her crew; this left, however, 38 unwounded men to be kept prisoners by the 15 remaining of the packet's complement. Fortunately, the privateer had been well provided with handcuffs and shackles for her expected prisoners; almost all the men of the WINDSOR CASTLE were posted round the hatchway of the *Jeune-Richard*; and the prisoners were called up one by one and each put in irons as he appeared.

The action had lasted almost the whole day, but there was little hope of rest. Commander Rogers divided his remaining fifteen men between his two ships and brought them both triumphantly into Barbados.

This was the most fiercely contested naval engagement of the whole of the wars. In no other case is the total of casualties more than half of the total of combatants.* One reason may be that privateers, especially in the West Indies, were reckoned to be no better than pirates in their treatment of prisoners, particularly if wounded; there was therefore more cause to fight desperately rather than surrender. But above everything stands out the character of Acting Commander William Rogers, who showed all the virtues of the greatest captains. Not only did he inspire his men to resist apparently hopeless odds; he arranged for the destruction of his mails in case of failure, at the same time he was planning the heroic coup which won the fight. Such conduct cannot be excelled. As usual when the enemy was a privateer, there were no promotions nor honours for the victor. Proabaly Rogers was not particularly disappointed; not in every naval officer burns the fiery ambition of a Nelson or a Cochrane, and there are many – many I have met! – who are satisfied to do their duty, and do it well.

* But see ANTELOPE and ATLANTE, page 52, chapter 3.

11

The Wolverine

During the early period when every novelty was welcomed, a Captain Schank came up with an invention to allow all the guns of a small ship to fire on the same side. Until then there had been one gun at each port, and consequently only half of the guns carried could be used at the same time, except on those very rare occasions when a ship was engaged on both sides at the same time; and then there were usually not enough men to work both sides simultaneously. It was worth while to try Captain Schank's idea, naturally as cheaply as possible.

A bark-rigged merchant ship, the RATTLER, 286 tons, was purchased, renamed the WOLVERINE, and rated as a 14-gun brig-sloop. As armed by Captain Schank she carried four 12-pounder carronades on her quarter-deck and one on her forecastle, quite ordinary; but her main deck carried two long 18-pounders and six 24-pounder carronades, each mounted on its gun-carriage on a heavy pivot. Eight ports were cut on each side, and grooves were cut in the deck to fit the wheels of the gun-carriages, so that all eight guns could be quite readily run across from one side to the other. Conservative persons shook their heads over the idea of running 15 tons from one side of a ship to the other, and pointed out that she could only fight from the lee side of an enemy, so that the weight of the wind on the sails would counteract the weight of her whole battery on one side; and thus voluntarily to give up the weather gauge was against Naval tradition. However, the idea of a small sloop bringing a couple of long 18s into action was very attractive. With a crew of 70 men under Commander Lewis Mortlock she was attached to the Channel Fleet.

Cruising off Boulogne on the 4th January 1799 in thick weather, the WOLVERINE discovered two large luggers close in to windward. In those waters luggers could scarcely be any other than French privateers, which in fact they were, the *Furet* and the *Rusé,* of fourteen and eight 4-pounders respectively, and each with 70 or 80 men. To encourage them to come closer, Commander Mortlock showed Danish colours, and the *Furet* came so close that her bowsprit projected over the WOLVERINE's quarter-deck. Immediately Commander Mortlock ordered British colours to be hoisted, lashed the bowsprit to his mizzen-chains with his own hands, and ordered to open fire.

Unable to bring her broadside to bear, the *Furet* had nothing for it but to try boarding, and her men came pouring onto the WOLVERINE's quarter-deck with great vigour, but were with difficulty repulsed. Meanwhile the *Rusé* came up on the other side, and boarded by the forecastle, so furiously that practically the whole crew had to leave the guns to repel this new invasion. While they were so occupied, some of the men of the *Furet* boarded again, and one man leapt up on the roof of the round-house encouraging his comrades. Commander Mortlock came rushing from forwards, the Frenchman put a pistol to his face and pressed the trigger, the pistol missed fire, and Mortlock pushed the Frenchman overboard with a thrust of his pike.

The *Furet* now set the WOLVERINE on fire by throwing bags of combustibles in through the cabin windows, and while the ship's company were engaged with this new assault both luggers made away. As they left, the *Furet* fired a parting shot which mortally wounded the Commander. Losses on the WOLVERINE were 10 casualties, of the luggers between 30 and 40.

The indecisive nature of this combat was due to the error of judgment on the part of the British commander in lashing the

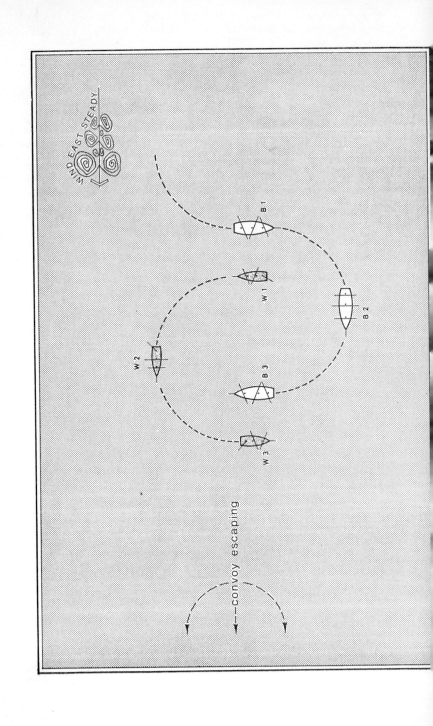

Furet to his rigging and thus making a boarding action inevitable against an enemy with more than twice his numbers. Had he stood off and engaged with gunfire, his two long 18s alone could have sunk both luggers if they did not surrender, and his six 24-pound carronades had at least equal range with the little 4-pounders of the enemy, with a really devastating effect. It would appear that Commander Mortlock had not been given a course in the tactical use of the unusual little ship he was to command.

The next action in which the WOLVERINE was engaged was in consort with the ARROW, as described in Chapter 14. In this action the ARROW was commanded by Nathaniel Portlock, and the WOLVERINE by William Bolton, who better understood the capacity of his vessel. Anchoring 70 yards from his Dutch opponent, with a spring on his cable, he could have brought his six big carronades into action as well as his long 18s if the *Gier* had not surrendered at the first shot.

On 24th March 1804 the WOLVERINE, under Commander Henry Gordon, was well out in the Atlantic escorting a convoy of eight merchantmen to Newfoundland. The wind was fair from the east, and in this direction were descried two large sail, bearing down on the convoy. By 2.30 p.m. it was clear that they were enemies, and the WOLVERINE, signalling the convoy to get away as best they could, turned to meet the strangers. One of them took no part in the encounter and has not been identified; the other was the *Blonde,* formerly a 24-gun ship-corvette of the French Navy, now a privateer, of about 600 tons and 240 men, with 30 guns, the main battery being twenty-four long 8-pounders on the main deck.

W 1 WOLVERINE lies-to, while the convoy makes its escape. B 1 *Blonde* comes up and engages WOLVERINE, but finds cannonade hotter than expected. She therefore sets sail and crosses the stern of the WOLVERINE, to engage her from the other side (B 2). W 2 This the WOLVERINE can by no means accept, and crosses the bow of the *Blonde,* in order to engage her from the only side which her peculiar armament admits (W 3 and B 3), which position is maintained until the end of the engagement.

At 4 p.m. the *Blonde* was well within range and the WOLVERINE hove-to on the starboard tack to give the *Blonde* a broadside; the *Blonde* hauled to the wind heading south, fired her broadside, and then wore again to pass the stern of the WOLVERINE, intending to rake her and come up on her lee side. This the WOLVERINE could not permit, for apart from a possibly disastrous raking fire in the stern, owing to her peculiar armament she could only engage from leeward; she therefore had to wear also, when the *Blonde* hove-to on the larboard beam of the WOLVERINE, to windward, and opened a heavy fire with musketry as well as the great guns, at less than pistol-shot distance. The WOLVERINE had now her desired position to leeward, but before she could fire, all her main guns had to be trundled across to the larboard side, and in doing so one of her two 18-pounders jumped the grooves and became hopelessly jammed, not only useless but a hindrance to the working of the other guns. When the other guns were in position a spirited fire was opened in spite of all handicaps, not the least of which was the fact that being heeled away from her antagonist she exposed a good deal of the underwater section of her hull.

The WOLVERINE was now incapable of further manoeuvre, could not in duty abandon her convoy and therefore could not try to escape by sailing away, even if that were possible; there was nothing for it but to hammer away at the hopelessly unequal battle, merely to give the convoy the longest possible time in which to escape. For nearly an hour the WOLVERINE kept up her resistance, until a fifth of her crew were casualties, her sails and rigging cut to pieces, many shot taken between wind and water, and her hold full of water, when she surrendered. No sooner had the *Blonde* taken off all the crew as prisoners than the WOLVERINE heeled and sank, thus proving, if proof was needed, that she had been fought to the last.

The loss of the WOLVERINE was taken rather badly by the great British public, who could not imagine that a privateer could be more than twice as powerful as a King's Ship; indeed, the *Annual Register* referred to the *Blonde* as 'a paltry privateer'. However, she was captured in the same area in August of that year by the 38-gun frigate LOIRE, Captain Frederick Maitland, with some trouble, and her actual force was ascertained. Admiralty had no doubts as to the merit of the action; although a prisoner of war, Commander Gordon was promoted post captain, and the name WOLVERINE was continued in the Royal Navy.*

The WOLVERINE was the last attempt to pull a magical quart out of a pint pot. Compared with the French, the ships were still over-gunned and under-manned; but the Navy had done with trick ships.

---

* In the same waters during the Second Great War, the destroyer HMS WOLVERINE, Captain James Rowland, D.S.O. and bar, in command of a small flotilla, performed notable service escorting the Halifax convoy.

12

Mutiny

As is generally known, there were two Fleet mutinies in 1797, one at Spithead and the other at the Nore. The former was settled within a month, among demonstrations of fervent loyalty by the mutineers. They had received all their demands about rations, pay and so on; there had been dismissed an admiral, four captains, and 54 other officers, commissioned and warrant; and a general amnesty was decreed and scrupulously observed. The mutiny at the Nore was a more serious business. A president, Richard Parker, had come to the fore, and had taken upon himself the pomp and circumstance of an admiral; there was suspicion of communication with the enemy, and definite threats to take the Fleet over to France, Ireland or America. When the mutiny was quelled Parker was courtmartialed and hanged within six weeks of the outbreak, and 412 of his supporters were courtmartialed later, of whom 29 were hanged, 9 flogged, 29 imprisoned and the rest pardoned.

Amongst those who got off scot-free was one Jackson, who had acted throughout the mutiny as secretary to Parker. He was obviously a literate person and was also a competent seaman, as were indeed most of the 'delegates' of the mutineers. Early in 1800 he was captain of the foretop in the DANAÉ, 20 guns, 9-pounders, Captain Lord Proby.

Early in 1800 the DANAÉ was one of the 'close inshore' squadron of the fleet engaged in the blockade of Brest; the squadron consisting of the 38-gun frigate LOIRE, Captain Newman, and four smaller ships. On 6th February they captured the fine French frigate *Pallas,* 38 guns, which was trying to make the port, and later a few merchantmen, so that all the ships of the squadron had a number of French prisoners on board, and a number of the most reliable seamen had been detached as prize crews.

On 14th March 1800 the DANAÉ chased the 16-gun brig-corvette *Colombe,* which, however, escaped and anchored in Camaret Bay under the guns of Fort Conquête, while the DANAÉ cruised hungrily around the entrance to the bay. This was the moment for which Jackson had been waiting. He had been preaching the seditious doctrines of the Nore mutineers to his shipmates, and being, like most mutiny leaders, much better educated than the usual foremast hand, he had found a considerable following. After dark on the 15th March, at 9.30 p.m., aided by his partisans he released the French prisoners and rushed the quarter-deck, where the only officer was the sailing master. They struck him down, with a serious cutlass wound in the head, threw him down the main hatchway, and battened down the grating, placing two boats weighted with shot on top of the grating. Thus if by any means the grating could have been cut through from below, the boats with their loads of shot would have fallen on the heads underneath.

All the officers were in their cots except Lord Proby and the officer of Marines. They attempted to make their way to the deck by the after hatchway, but found it heavily guarded; Lord Proby was wounded in the head by a cutlass and forced down, while the hatchway was secured. They now took stock of the situation. Besides the officers, 40 of the crew remained loyal, but all the arms they could muster amounted to ten cutlasses, four muskets, and a few pistols; in any case, they were so securely battened down that there was no possibility of any attempt to re-take the ship. However they were in control of all the stores, and they could hope that if the weather held the ship would have to hold off to sea, and when the ready provisions were exhausted the mutineers would have to make some move. Unfortunately the wind changed, and next morning, the 16th March, the DANAÉ ran in Camaret Bay and anchored alongside the *Colombe.*

Jackson now sent the jolly-boat to apprise the captain of the *Colombe* of the situation, and shortly the first lieutenant, with an armed party, came on board the DANAÉ and asked Lord Proby if he surrendered; the reply was 'To the French nation but not to mutineers.' Both ships now made for Brest. For some hours they were followed by two powerful British frigates, the ANSON, 44, Captain Durham, and the BOADICEA, 38, Captain Keats; but Jackson made the correct answering signals, and the captains concluded that this was a British ship chasing a French brig, with which she was obviously well able to cope; so they stood away. Lord Proby, however, took advantage of this distraction of attention to weight the box containing the private signals and heave it out of a cabin window.

On the 17th the two ships arrived at Brest, where Jackson and his confederates were horrified to find that they were treated like any other prisoner ratings and all marched off to Dinan prison, while the officers whom they had handed over were treated with the utmost consideration. In October 1798 a squadron from Brest had been engaged with a British squadron off Lough Swilly in Ireland and several of the French ships were captured, including the frigate *Bellone,* Captain Louis-Leon Jacob. He had been very properly treated by his captors, duly exchanged, and was now waiting at Brest for another command. He was very happy to repay hospitality, and in particular enabled them to pay their way by very handsomely exchanging their Bank of England paper for French gold. On his suggestion Admiral Bruix allowed most of the officers to return to England, on parole not to serve until regularly exchanged. Later Lord

Proby stood court-martial for the loss of his ship and was honourably acquitted.

Far different was the case of the mutineers. The brief Peace of Amiens two years later brought release to all prisoners of war, but they had nowhere to go. Mutiny, even in the sense of refusing to obey an order, was a hanging matter; but mercy might be sought. There was no possibility of mercy for mutineers who had wounded two officers and handed their ship over to the enemy. Nothing remained for their lifetime but a miserable Ishmaelite kind of existence. Some might take French service; some might make their way to Bordeaux and sign on some of the many American merchantmen which used that port; but always there was the possibility of a British warship closing in and a smart lieutenant coming aboard with his armed boat's crew to look for deserters. One thing was certain: they had alienated themselves for life from their friends, their families and their native land.

13

Commander Maurice
and His Unsinkable Sloop

Martinique was the principal French colony in the West Indies, a sizeable island of some 400 square miles, bigger than any of the British West Indian islands. At Fort de France, the capital, it had a magnificent harbour, fit to accommodate the largest fleet; on the west coast near the southern end, it was sheltered from the prevailing easterly winds and yet accessible in all weathers except hurricanes. The harbour was so heavily fortified as to be impregnable from seaward, and every possible landing beach on the island was covered by cannon, nearly 300 heavy guns being allocated to the island's defence; there was also an infantry force of about 2,500 regulars, and about the same number of local militia. Such a harbour was invaluable. Here merchant men could assemble in safety until the Atlantic was more or less clear, or could run for shelter if chased. Every kind of warship could take on stores, refresh its crew, and wait to pounce on any possible prey, with a safe refuge if unsuccessful.

The extreme SW corner of Martinique is Diamond Point, about five miles south of the entrance to Fort de France harbour; and a mile offshore lies, or rather stands, the Diamond Rock, a shaft of volcanic origin standing right up out of the sea from out of fair depths. It is very similar to the Bass Rock at the entrance of the Firth of Forth, although somewhat

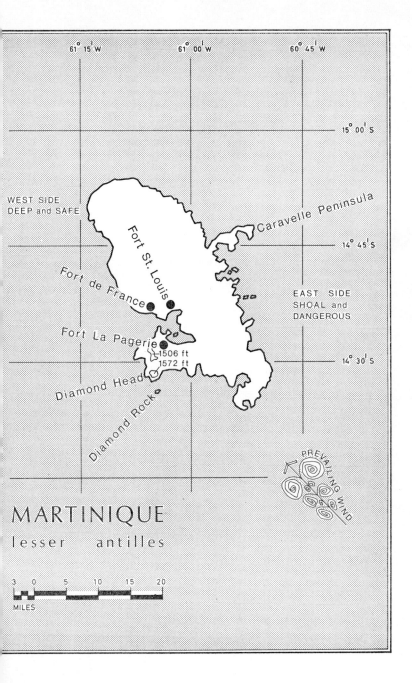

WEST SIDE
DEEP and SAFE

Caravelle Peninsula

Fort St. Louis

Fort de France

EAST SIDE
SHOAL and
DANGEROUS

Fort La Pagerie

1506 ft
1572 ft

Diamond Head

Diamond Rock

PREVAILING WIND

MARTINIQUE
lesser   antilles

3 0   5   10   15   20

MILES

H

higher, about 600 feet; as on the Bass, the cliffs rise perpendicularly out of the sea, and the rock is quite inaccessible on all sides except at a place on the west where a landing is practicable in suitable weather. The route slopes obliquely upwards through broken and dangerous ground to the NW side, whence a steep wooded ascent leads to the summit. Unlike the Bass, the Diamond Rock has no spring of water, and was uninhabited.

At the end of 1803 the British line-of-battle ship CENTAUR, 74, Captain Murray Maxwell, having on board Commodore Samuel Hood, was cruising off Fort de France to intercept all passage whether in or out. It was found that those of the French who knew the area used to dodge around the Diamond Rock and often escape thereby into Fort de France. To prevent this, and make the rock a danger instead of a refuge to the French, Commodore Hood decided to take possession and fortify it, thus denying to the French the strait between the rock and the point.

There was no opposition from the enemy, to whom such an idea had never occurred; there was only the silent resistence of the rock and of gravitation. A 24-pounder gun weighs $2\frac{1}{2}$ tons, and to manhandle such a dead weight up a 600-foot cliff was a task to be attempted only by such accomplished officers as Samuel Hood and Murray Maxwell* and the men they had trained. The ship moored at a convenient distance off the rock, and an anchor cable was rigged from the deck to the top of the rock. Running on the cable was a large pulley, from which the gun was suspended, so that the cable took part of the weight and kept the gun clear of any obstruction; the actual hauling was done by two hawsers attached to the gun, with a hundred men on each. In this way not only the guns but the gun-carriages, ammunition and all stores were safely landed. The principle is now of course well known and commonly applied, but it was new in 1803.

* *The Frigates*, page 168.

Five heavy guns were landed, three 24-pounders and two 18s. One of the 24s covered the landing-place and a wide area as well, one was on the NE side commanding the strait between the rock and the point, and one was more than half way up the rock looking towards the entrance of Fort de France harbour. Although far out of range of the harbour any ship entering or leaving from east or south had to give it a wide berth. The two 18s were mounted on the summit of the rock, with an all-round field of fire; the view over the sea from this point was extremely wide, and there was a little disappointment that the range of the guns was not similarly enhanced. A good supply of powder and shot was landed, with small arms and ammunition for 120 men, and provisions and water for four months. An armed launch was provided for such allies as might offer. Lieutenant James Wilkes Maurice of the CENTAUR was promoted commander of this stout vessel, which was duly registered in the Navy List as HM Sloop of War DIAMOND ROCK, as from January 1804.

The crew of the new sloop had a wonderful time: they were freed from the perils of the sea, and also of the enemy, for the French had nothing bigger than a frigate in the West Indies, and even a frigate dared not venture within range of the plunging fire from the Rock's heavy guns; a single shot from such a height would plunge through all the decks and the bottom of a ship, either sinking her at once or putting her out for a lengthy repair. No ship could use the channel inside the Rock, while the launch could pounce out by night on any un-suspecting merchantman bound for the complete safety of Fort de France. Moreover, as well as an extraordinary field of view the British had an equal field of vision for their signals. They reported every ship and every movement they saw, whether or not there was any ship in the vicinity to receive the signal; and the French on shore could never tell. The occupation of Diamond Rock might be only a preliminary to a large-scale invasion of Martinique itself.

The 13th of May 1805 brought a busy day not only for the

lookouts but for the gunners. A great fleet passed HMS DIAMOND ROCK and anchored in Fort de France harbour, consisting of eleven French and five Spanish line-of-battle ships, seven frigates, and six lesser vessels, to all of which the British paid iron tribute as they passed. During the night another French 74 came in, and on the 16th a big Spanish 80-gun ship. For her the DIAMOND ROCK hoisted French colours, so that she came close alongside, when the colours were quickly changed and the Spaniard received an unexpected salvo to hasten her on her way into Fort de France harbour.

This was Admiral Villeneuve with the French Toulon Fleet, who had successfully lured Nelson and the Mediterranean Fleet to the West Indies, and was now to return to Europe, pick up the fleets from Ferrol and Brest, proceed with overwhelming numbers into the Channel and give Napoleon command of the 'damned ditch' for the three days he needed to make himself master of the world. For reasons never fully explained, Villeneuve remained for the rest of the month of May in Fort de France harbour. He may have been waiting for information about Nelson's movements, or it may be that the bombardment from the Rock had necessitated repairs; at any rate the Admiral decided not to take his fleet out until the threat from the DIAMOND ROCK had been eliminated.

For this service he detailed a formidable squadron, consisting of two 74-gun ships of the line, a frigate, a corvette and a schooner, with eleven gunboats, and nearly 400 regular infantry. This force sailed from Fort de France harbour on the 29th May 1805, but owing to the prevailing winds it was the 31st before it got to windward of the sloop and was in a position to attack.

Seeing the force which was approaching, Commander Maurice decided that he could not hold the landing-place nor the lower guns; so he scuttled the launch, spiked the two lower guns, and prepared to defend the higher part of the Rock. For three days the ships bombarded the works with more than 200 guns, while the infantry forced ashore at the landing-place, losing three gun-boats and two rowing boats full of soldiers.

Meanwhile the powder on the DIAMOND ROCK was running low, and the provisions and water for four months, which had been put on board in January of the previous year, had been replenished from time to time, but a fresh supply was overdue and no supply ship could approach. Commander Maurice thought it best to talk terms while he could at least make a show of renewed resistance, and put out a flag of truce. The French were quick to respond, and the schooner came in with a similar flag and a senior officer. Very honourable terms were soon arranged, officers to retain their swords, men to march out under their officers' orders, the company to be taken to Fort de France and thence by the first available cartel to the most convenient British ship or base, without further conditions. It would appear that Admiral Villeneuve was extremely anxious to have this outpost abandoned.

Out of 107 remaining men on the Rock, the losses in this last engagement were only two killed and one wounded in the sloop's company; the French loss was certainly very heavy, but has never been stated from their side, so that there are only estimates : none from the French naval commander, a 'hasty calculation' by the commander of the landing troops of about 50 casualties among his men, the estimate of Commander Maurice of about 70 casualties in the landed force, plus the five large boats sunk by gunfire and whatever casualties were suffered among the bombarding warships.

The following day, 4th June 1805, Admiral Villeneuve with all his fleet sailed unchallenged past the Diamond Rock, bound for Basse-Terre and Europe.

Commander Maurice stood his court-martial for the loss of his sloop DIAMOND ROCK, and was not only honourably acquitted but highly commended for his firm and judicious conduct, which was, indeed, not forgotten six years later, when a somewhat similar command was vacant, but Maurice was by then a post captain, so *that* story must be told elsewhere.

14

The Arrow and the Dart

There was no lack of experimental building in the early part of the wars, especially when Jeremy Bentham was Inspector-General of all naval works, for he rather fancied himself as a naval architect and saw no reason to look to French models for all improvements when he could do better himself. He had no difficulty in having his designs carried out so long as he restricted himself to sloops and below; my Lords Commissioners were strangely conservative when it came to frigates and ships of the line.

In 1796 two sloops to Bentham's designs were ordered, and put in commission at the end of the same year. They were 386 tons each, and much more resembled a rich yachtsman's ship of 1870 than a warship of 1796. They had considerable overhangs both forward and aft, their breadth was much less than usual for their length, and instead of the usual tumblehome of all gun-carrying vessels of the period, their breadth increased from the waterline to the deck. The idea was that as they heeled more and more flotation would be presented at the waterline, which was in fact true, but it was the bulk below the waterline that mattered more, the metacentric shelf was too high. This was met by setting the guns very low and adding to the deadwood of the keel, so that eventually they turned out to be very stiff and fast. Their armament was enormous, all

32-pounder carronades, 24 on the main deck and two on each of forecastle and quarter-deck; later the DART added another two on the quarter-deck. This gave a weight of shot, at carronade range, equal to the main battery of the VICTORY and far greater than the most powerful frigate; but sloops they were and sloops they remained, to be commanded not by a post captain but by a commander.

The idea behind the ARROW and the DART was to produce a very fast ship with a very powerful short-range armament, which could easily escape from a more powerful or longer-ranged ship, or else bring to close action any ship she could tackle. Unfortunately, owing to the 'exigencies of the Service' – euphemism for the stupidity of superiors – neither had much opportunity to demonstrate their particular capabilities.

The great victory off Camperdown in 1797 had assured Britain the command of the North Sea, and it was very seldom thereafter that the Dutch came out in any strength, remaining among the shoals and dangerous channels of the Texel. On the 9th September 1799 Vice-Admiral Mitchell, cruising offshore with a strong squadron, had information of a ship and a brig in the outer channels, and detached in search of them the ARROW and the small WOLVERINE, also an experimental ship, Commanders Portlock and Bolton (Chapter 11). The ARROW was not the ideal ship for this mudlarking, having a fairly deep draught, 12 feet 8 inches, for her tonnage, but by careful seamanship and the aid of some Dutch pilots they were able to nose their way in, slithering over the flats on the flood tide and finding some channel on the ebb. At length, on the 12th, they found the vessels they sought, moored in an advantageous position in a narrow channel near Harlingen. The brig was nearer, and Commander Portlock ordered the WOLVERINE to engage her, while he passed on to meet the much larger ship beyond.

The WOLVERINE came boldly up, anchored very neatly, and fired one preliminary shot; whereupon the Dutchman fired three guns to leeward and hauled down her colours. She turned out to be the *Gier*, with fourteen long 12-pounders and 80 men. Commander Bolton took her pilot and sent him aboard the ARROW, whose Dutch pilots had refused to take her any further. The ship the ARROW was now to engage was said to be the *Draak*, Lieutenant Van Esch, oddly but heavily armed with six brass howitzers, 50-pounders, two long 32s and sixteen long 18-pounders. As the ARROW worked her way with difficulty against wind and tide in the narrow channel she came under heavy fire from the long guns of the *Draak*, which her crew had to endure as best they might for twenty minutes before they got within carronade range. At last they came abreast, and the ARROW opened fire with her mighty broadside of 32-pound shot, while the *Draak* fired her howitzers, which appeared to be loaded with langridge; the enemy did not attempt to reload them, but kept on firing with one 32 and eight 18s against the ARROW's broadside of fourteen 32s, which could be fired at almost twice the rate of the long guns. This could not go on for long: after a quarter of an hour the WOLVERINE was seen approaching and the *Draak* surrendered. Casualties were light, one killed and nine wounded in the ARROW, and apparently only two killed and three wounded in the *Draak*; but it subsequently transpired that many of her casualties had been sent in by boat to Harlingen, under cover of the gun-smoke. She was fired by her captors, being an old ship in poor order; but the *Gier*, a new brig of 324 tons, was taken into the Royal Navy.

While advancing, both the ARROW and the WOLVERINE flew, as well as the British ensign, the orange flag of Nassau, which was hauled down before action commenced. It transpired that the ready surrender of the *Gier* was due to a reluctance of the crew to fire on the orange flag. This had already been exemplified a fortnight earlier, when a whole Dutch battle fleet had surrendered to a British fleet flying the orange flag with the British and having a proclamation from the Prince of Orange; the officers were willing to fight it out for their honour, but the crews mutinied and refused to fight. They were just as brave as the men who had fought at Camperdown, but they didn't like the way that Holland was becoming a satellite of the French Republic. The Dutch, of all nations, like to know what they are fighting about; the reason why.

At the commencement of 1805 the ARROW was in the Mediterranean, based at Malta, her commander now Richard Budd Vincent. In January she was detailed, along with the bomb-ketch ACHERON, Commander Arthur Farquhar, to escort a convoy of 35 merchantmen to England. It would have been difficult to have found two less suitable ships for convoy duties. The ARROW relied upon her speed to run out of trouble, or to bring her formidable carronades within range; but what use was her speed when she was tethered to the lumbering convoy? As for the bomb-ketch, she was built for one purpose only: to toss big explosive shells into stationary targets such as towns or anchored fleets. Her mortars were useless against a moving target, and her other guns gave her less fire-power than the smallest brig. A proper escort would have been two frigates or an old line-of-battle ship, but nothing such could be spared; Nelson had only two frigates with the Mediterranean Fleet, and as for ships of the line! Everybody knew that the crunch was coming, that 1805 must see the decisive action which would determine whether Napoleon was to dictate his terms from St James's or be repulsed for ever from the shores of the Island.

On the 17th January 1805 the French fleet in Toulon put to sea, with eleven of the line and seven frigates, with orders to pass through the Straits of Gibraltar, pick up as many Spanish allies as might be ready for sea, and proceed to the West Indies. However, two days out a violent storm scattered and damaged the fleet, which returned to Toulon with two battleships disabled and two frigates missing, the *Hortense* and the *Incorruptible*; these had weathered the storm very well, and were cruising about east of Gibraltar waiting for the fleet or further orders. These were new frigates of the most powerful types, the *Hortense* rated as 40 guns but actually mounting 48, the

The Arrow and the Dart 121

Incorruptible rated as 38 but mounting 42; both had crews of 340 to 350, plus 300 soldiers on each.

At dawn on the 3rd February 1805 Commander Vincent sighted Cape Caxine on the African coast about thirty miles to the south, and kept on his course for the Straits, W by N, with a light breeze from the NE. The ARROW was leading the convoy, now 34 ships, one having been lost in a storm, and the ACHERON was covering the rear when she descried two large sails to the eastward, sailing on much the same course as the convoy. This was reported to the ARROW, which acknowledged the signal. At 10.30 a.m. Commander Vincent ordered the ACHERON to investigate the strangers, and at 11.15 a.m. Commander Farquhar signalled that the ships looked suspicious and were large frigates. Commander Vincent now left the head of the convoy and ordered it to be led by the DUCHESS OF RUTLAND, the most like a warship of all the motley fleet; they had been sailing in two lines fairly well apart and were now ordered to close up. At 12.30 p.m. the ACHERON showed her colours and fired a gun; as the frigates made no reply there could be no further doubt that they were enemies. On this Commander Vincent ordered the convoy to make all sail for Gibraltar, and signalled the ACHERON to join him, which she was not able to do until 4.30 p.m. owing to the very light and uncertain wind. At 5 p.m. it fell dead calm. The two commanders now had a conference and decided to remain between the convoy and the French frigates, both the convoy and the enemy being about five miles from the escort.

Up to this time there had been uncertainty on the French side as to what precisely they had met. It might even have been Nelson himself with the Mediterranean Fleet! The apparent detachment of two small vessels to reconoitre them did nothing to contradict this possibility; but when they saw the main body crowding on all sail to get away, and observed the clumsy disarray of the ships, no doubt was left; it was a large convoy with a very weak escort, a gift from heaven. The calm was a pity, but it affected all ships alike, and only delayed the capture for a few hours. One thing was dubious, whether to take the prizes into Cartagena or risk it for Toulon.

The frigates, with their fine lines and great sail power, were able to ghost a little during the night, and when a very light air came up from the SW at 11 p.m. they were only three miles from the escort and less than seven from the convoy. The ARROW and the ACHERON were in close line ahead, but the frigates were fairly widely separated. Shortly after 4 a.m. on the 4th February the *Hortense* passed to leeward of the ARROW without firing, but on coming abreast of the ACHERON opened fire on her rigging, causing considerable damage but no casualties; the French wanted their prize as intact as possible. The ACHERON fired her pitiful little starboard broadside of four guns, then went about and fired the larboard ones, without any observed effect. At 5.30 a.m. the *Incorruptible* came up and passed both British ships without firing, although the ACHERON fired two guns at fairly long range.

Dawn came at 6 a.m., with a very light wind from the NW. The two frigates were seen between the escort and the convoy, in line ahead going south, the *Hortense* flying a broad pendant to denote the commodore. The ARROW now signalled the DUCHESS OF RUTLAND to engage the enemy, which signal was neither acknowledged nor obeyed. The DUCHESS looked rather like an old 44 or 50-gun two-decker, and had some guns, so that at least a show of entering the combat might have made the frigates hesitate; but she kept on westward with the convoy leaving the escort to its fate.

What that fate was could not be a matter of doubt, only of time. By skilfully drawing the British fire during the brief night encounter the French had satisfied themselves that both were armed only with carronades; the sloop could not have more than 28 of these, and the bomb-ketch 8. The complement of a sloop was 125 men and boys, and of a ketch 67; a total of 36 carronades and 192 men and boys, plus passengers in the ARROW, seven male invalids, two females and an infant. The British very well knew the classes and force of the frigates;

the *Hortense* with 48 guns, the *Incorruptible* with 42, mostly long 18-pounders, only 8 out of the 90 being carronades; and a total complement including soldiers of about 1,300 men. To engage such an overwhelming force was mere suicide; but if the convoy was to escape, suicide appeared to be necessary.

The French ships lay between the convoy and the escort, headed south in the waft from the NW, while the convoy beat up to windward. The ARROW now made sail on the starboard tack, the ACHERON followed her closely, and they sailed westward to the attack. The frigates now sailed eastward to meet them, to engage to leeward. At 7.30 a.m. the action commenced, the *Incorruptible,* leading, passing the ARROW and giving her a broadside *en passant*; to which the ARROW replied, thus necessarily giving the range of her carronades while the *Incorruptible* sailed ahead to engage the ACHERON. The *Hortense* now engaged the ARROW, keeping almost out of the effective range of her carronades while smashing her through and through with long 18-pounders.

The ships slowly passed each other in the light air, and when out of shot the French went about and returned to the attack, the *Hortense* now leading. The ARROW turned into the wind, intending to present her broadside to the approaching prows, hoping to get in at least one raking broadside for each of them; but what with the very light wind and her crippled rigging, she did not answer the helm, and received the whole broadside of the *Hortense* in her starboard quarter, without being able to make any effective reply. The *Hortense* now pushed on after the ACHERON, leaving the ARROW to be finished off by the *Incorruptible*. This, however, was neither quick nor easy. Without hope and without fear, Commander Vincent and his men carried on the fight for nearly an hour, when, with a third of his men killed or wounded, all the rigging shot to pieces, the steering disabled, four guns dismounted, and many shot below the waterline, Commander Vincent ordered the colours to be struck.

The ACHERON resisted for twenty minutes longer, for those

bomb vessels were so strongly built to carry their mortars that they could take a tremendous hammering. For more than an hour she carried on this extraordinary fight of 8 guns and 67 men against 48 guns and 650 men until she was nearly shot to pieces, when Commander Farquhar ordered the ensign to be hauled down.

Both the British ships had all their boats shot to flinders, so that the French had to get out their boats to bring off all the prisoners. No sooner had all the people been taken off the ARROW than she turned on her side and sank. The ACHERON did not sink, but she was such a wreck as to be useless as a prize, and the French set her on fire.

The delay was vital for the convoy; of the 34 ships only 3 were captured by the French, including the DUCHESS OF RUTLAND, which had forfeited honour without gaining safety. It was the old story, so often repeated in the annals of the Navy : the warships must sacrifice themselves so that the convoy may get through. The action was properly appreciated by Admiralty, and both commanders were promoted post captains while they were still prisoners of war. Never was the discipline of the Royal Navy better vindicated than in this action; no hare-brained rushing on unconsidered odds, but a cold acceptance of certain defeat and probable death, pursuant to orders. In all the long account of the Price of Admiralty there is no more glorious defeat than the ARROW and ACHERON.

15

The Dart

Dunkirk has long been famous in British history. From Tudor times it was noted as a nest of pirates and privateers, with ships of surprising speed and handiness which could swoop out from their strategic position, gather up a scoop of prizes in the Straits, and be safely back within their sands and shoals before any effective action could be taken against them. Cromwell had taken it from the Spaniards, as an ally of the French; Charles II had sold it to Louis XIV. Although it could not serve for ships of the line, as could the Scheldt and the Texel, it was a perpetual nuisance to all the small British ships passing the Dover Straits to or from London River and the harbours of the east coast.

In 1800 there lay in Dunkirk four French frigates, much larger vessels than commonly used the port, but as they had got in they could come out, and such a strong squadron could not be tolerated on the very doorpost of Britain's gateway. Accordingly, in June 1800 there was assembling a motley squadron of two small frigates and fifteen smaller vessels, under the command of Captain Henry Inman, to winkle them out. Difficulties arose; no pilots could be found who would undertake to bring the frigates into Dunkirk, although the French ships already there were much larger and deeper in draught. Even for sloops it was impossible to find local pilots, the fact being that everybody who knew the sands was engaged in the smuggling traffic, and dared not give mortal offence to the Dunkirkers. At length it was decided to smoke them out with fireships, and a squadron was made up thus: the DART, Commander Patrick Campbell; gun-brigs BOXER and BITER, Lieutenants Norman and Gilbert; hired cutters KENT and ANN, Lieutenants Cooban and Young; and four fireships. The master of the ANN volunteered to pilot the DART, the others to follow closely; and the night of the 7th July 1800 was chosen for this extraordinary venture, in which a light detachment from the outside squadron was to enter the port and drive out from their moorings four powerful frigates, which were more than a match for the whole of the squadron.

About midnight the DART sighted the French frigates moored in line ahead. As she approached, she was hailed in turn by the first two frigates, and replying in French was allowed to pass unmolested; the third, however, the *Incorruptible,* opened fire on the DART, which replied with double-shotted carronades. The close range suited the DART ideally, but without staying to fight it out she ranged on, laying out a stern anchor, and ran aboard of the last frigate, the *Désirée,* the DART's bowsprit passing between the forestay and the foremast. Instantly the first lieutenant, James McDermitt, leapt on the frigate's forecastle, followed by a division of seamen and Marines, and after a fierce encounter cleared the decks. He was wounded, however, and expecting the enemy to counterattack he asked for another officer and reinforcements. Meantime the cable of the stern anchor had been cut, allowing the DART to swing close alongside, so that the second lieutenant, William Pearce, with the second division was able to board by the quarter-deck and drive all the French below with heavy losses. Immediately Lieutenant Pearce cut the mooring cables, made sail on the *Désirée* and took her off over the sands on the top of the tide.

Meanwhile the fireships, well handled, had been set alight and steered for the frigates, which were also fired upon at short range by the DART, BOXER and BITER; but cutting their cables and setting sail the French made off downwind through the channels to safety. One went ashore on the Braak sand, but was got off next tide and the three frigates eventually returned safely to their original anchorage.

The difference in the losses was most remarkable. In this fierce boarding action the DART had only one man killed and eleven wounded, while the *Désirée*, with nearly three times the number of crew, had over a hundred killed and wounded, including nearly every officer; exemplifying once again that in the confined area of a deck total numbers do not matter nearly so much as the fighting qualities of the front rank. Speed and ferocity are the essentials; the slow and half-hearted are better elsewhere.

The *Désirée*, a fine new frigate of 1,015 tons, was taken into the Royal Navy as a 36-gun frigate, and the command was given to Captain Inman, who had commanded the whole squadron. Commander Patrick Campbell was promoted to post captain and given command of the ARIADNE, a 20-gun post-ship of about half the force of the sloop he had to relinquish as below the dignity of a post captain. First Lieutenant McDermitt was promoted commander. Earlier in the war there would probably have been a frigate and a knighthood for the commander of such an action, but the public was growing a little blasé and saw nothing all that much out of the way in a sloop of 386 tons boarding a frigate of 1,015 tons and carrying her with the cutlass.

In the ARROW versus the *Incorruptible,* and the DART versus the *Désirée*, we have sister ships encountering sister ships with very different results, for reasons which are clearly due to whether or not a ship was employed for the duties for which she was designed. Had the ARROW encountered the *Incorruptible* casually on the high seas, she could no doubt have sailed away into safety; but she was tethered to her convoy, so that the frigate could lie out of accurate carronade range and batter the ARROW to pieces with her long guns. In the other case, the narrow channels between the sands enabled the DART to come close up, when her 32-pounder carronades were devastatingly effective and the moored *Désirée* was a set target for boarding. However the lesson was read, after the loss of the ARROW there were no more of her type constructed, although the DART had a long and honourable war service before being relegated to the Coastguard.

16

The Hard Way to a Commission

In the early days of the wars Admiralty was always open for experiment, thus creating new classes of very few ships. It was after experience was gained that the idea became fixed of as few classes as possible each with as many ships as possible; seldom attained, because of the inherent dislike for scrapping any obsolete ship so long as she floated.

In 1796 Admiralty purchased from the Honourable East India Company nine large ships, all built at Bombay of teak, from 1,170 to 1,430 tons; two-deckers, flush-built, without either quarter-deck or forecastle, making them very weatherly in high winds. The larger carried 56 guns, the smaller 54; 18-pounder long guns on the lower deck, 32-pounder carronades on the upper. They were rated as fourth-rate, but not for the line of battle. They were intended for a specific purpose : to act as flag-ships on the various stations in the West Indies. The teak would last better than oak in tropical waters and the armament was more than enough to meet any French frigate, while if ships of the line approached the flag-ship could draw under the guns of the shore forts. None of them saw much action, although the CALCUTTA, Captain Woodriff, during a homeward voyage in 1805 fell in with a French squadron off the Scillies and was captured; in 1809 the *Calcutta* was destroyed by the IMPERIEUSE, Captain Lord

Cochrane, during the action in the Basque Roads (*The Frigates,* Chapter 10.) The rest of the 54s and 56s were gradually phased out of service by that time.*

In all ships the great enemy is boredom. In a warship at sea, under a good captain, this foe may be met by strict attention to duty, constant vigilance and the changing conditions of weather and rig; but in harbour boredom got the upper hand, especially in flag-ships. Thus in 1796 one of the newly-purchased 54s, the ABERGAVENNY, Captain Henry Vansittart, was sent out as flag-ship to Port Royal, Jamaica. During the whole of 1797 and most of 1798 she swung at her moorings, without the least incident to relieve the tedium. The commodore and his staff were kept busy enough with the frigates, sloops, brigs and schooners under his command, which were constantly employed in collecting information, convoying merchant ships and capturing enemy ones, and continually fighting the enemy privateers and pirates which swarmed in those waters; but the officers of the flag-ship could only watch the little ships busily plying their office while they hung about on the moored flag-ship. Owing to the risk of infection on that fever-haunted island the ship had to lie well out, and for the same reason shore leave was almost impossible; they were thrown on their own resources, and after the first year these began to wear thin.

The usual grumble in the wardroom was that while the officers of the cruising ships were picking up prize-money, and the captain on the station had his share, the officers of the flag-ship had neither a part in others' pickings nor the opportunity to get any for themselves. At last the idea grew up – why should the flag-ship officers not get a little ship of their own, to be rated as tender to the flag-ship, and to cruise for prizes? The captain was approached and was quite agreeable – no doubt delighted that an occupation had been found for some of the company and an interest for all. He could not allow any of the

---

* The earnest student will observe that in 1814 56-gun flush-decked ships reappear in the Navy List. These were, however, quite different ships.

ship's boats to be used, but he would allow anybody to volunteer and would provide arms and ammunition. In a place like Port Royal, where prizes were being sold almost daily, almost any kind of small vessel was to be had, at a price. What the wardroom's funds could run to was a large frigate's launch, with a 1-pounder swivel gun mounted in the bows and fit to carry up to 30 men with provisions for a month.

The question now arose, who was to command her? A certain lack of enthusiasm was observed, as the officers pondered on exchanging their comfortable cots, well-served wardroom table and deck promenade for the cramped bare boards and hard fare of an open boat, perhaps for a month on end, and for what? Any prize-money won by the tender would be divided among the captain, officers and crew of the whole ship. Obviously the first lieutenant could not go, nor the signals lieutenant; there was an excuse for everybody, but a volunteer was found, Acting-Lieutenant Michael Fitton.

Fitton was no enthusiastic youngster but a most experienced seaman, who knew exactly what he was letting himself in for. He had nearly twenty years of service behind him, having come aft through the hawse-hole,* and was most competent in navigation as well as all the other duties of a naval officer. In spite of his 'age for rank' he was not at all the typical plodder but an active and ambitious man who chafed in the rather invidious rank of acting lieutenant. He wore the uniform, performed the duties and enjoyed the privileges of lieutenant's rank, but only during the captain's pleasure. His substantive rank was master's mate, and the only way to get his commission was by the recommendation of his captain after some meritorious service. Here was his chance.

Some financial arrangements had to be made: the wardroom agreed that out of any prize-money accruing, only half would be divided among the officers and the other half would go towards providing a bigger and better ship; the lower deck

* The term for promotion from the lower deck.

agreed that the volunteers for the launch would have half of the prize-money, and the non-combatants the other half among them. The captain issued powder and shot for the swivel, a few muskets, and a cutlass per man; the acting-lieutenant had his sword and pistols. Thus manned and armed the ABERGAVENNY's tender set forth to seek the enemy, surely the lightest and weakest warship ever sent out; about half the size and man-power of the Viking longships of eight hundred years earlier.

Fighting power, however, is always relative; a 1-pound gun could overawe a merchantman with no guns at all, and in a boarding action the discipline and dash of the man-o-war's men could always drive below the irresolute and ill-disciplined crew of a Spanish privateer. Prizes were brought in, prize-money accumulated, and at length Mr Fitton found himself command-ing a real seagoing ship, decked all over, the schooner FERRET, with six 3-pounder popguns and a crew of 45. Treading the deck of the ship under his command, Fitton felt that he could go anywhere and tackle everything.

The opportunity came. On 5th October 1799, while cruising off the NE of Jamaica, the FERRET sighted a larger schooner under British colours, having eight ports on each side. She didn't seem right, somehow. No 16-gun schooner was known in the Royal Navy, and both her ensign and pendant seemed to be far too big for the ship. The FERRET tacked to speak her, but keeping the weather gauge just in case; sure enough, as they drew close the stranger hoisted Spanish colours and opened fire. Mr Fitton knew quite well that this was a ship of much greater force than his; in fact, it was afterwards ascertained to be a Spanish privateer with fourteen long 6-pounders and a crew of at least 100; he had not the least idea, however, of doing anything other than engaging. The cannonade lasted for half an hour, when the Spaniard broke off and made sail to the NW, closely followed by the FERRET; so closely, in fact, that observers on shore, seeing the respective sizes of the schooners, concluded that the FERRET had been captured by the Spaniard and sent word overland to Captain Vansittart that he had lost his tender.

Far different was the fact. When the wind dropped after sunset Mr Fitton got out his sweeps, and at 11 p.m. came alongside the privateer and the contest was renewed. After half an hour a breeze came up, and the Spaniard made sail and put into the fortified harbour of Santiago de Cuba, having had 11 killed and 20 wounded. The FERRET had no casualties at all, but was badly cut about in the sails and rigging and had to return to Port Royal, not at all depressed, having engaged a ship of twice her manpower and nearly five times her gunpower, completely defeated her and chased her into harbour with heavy casualties.

During 1800 the accumulating prize-money allowed the purchase of an 8-gun schooner, named the ACTIVE, which then cruised far and wide throughout the Caribbean, sending in many prizes and destroying even more small but dangerous craft not worth the trouble of bringing into port. In December she returned to Port Royal and was scheduled for an extensive overhaul. To pass the time Acting-Lieutenant Fitton applied for and received permission to transfer himself and his well-tried crew to one of the prizes he had sent in, a Spanish felucca of 50 tons, not really big enough for her sonorous title of *Nostra Senora dos los Dolores,* easily enough shortened to 'Dolly'. She was an odd sort of vessel, flush-decked without any bulwarks and armed with a single 12-pounder, which was too heavy to carry in a firing position while under way. It sat on a traversing carriage on a screw-jack, by which it could be lowered into the hold or raised when it came into action. With her felucca rig and big disappearing gun she was the ideal pirate; nothing less British could be imagined. She was able to penetrate all the pirate's nests and be taken for one of themselves.

In January 1801 they set out for a cruise along the Caribbean coast of South America – the only area which can correctly be called the Spanish Main. They picked up and destroyed a number of small pirates and privateers, not worth sending in; but a few days of rough weather showed them that the felucca was not as staunch as they had supposed. Mr Fitton anchored off a small desert island, where he rigged a tent, landed his crew and stores, and hauled the ship ashore for examination. It was not encouraging; the deck leaked at every seam, keeping the men continuously wet and cold, for which they were so little prepared that nearly half of them were sick; the big beam on which the gun rested was badly sprung, and it was obvious that it would stand very little more gun-raising; the sails were torn and the rigging in poor condition, but there were no spare sails or rope. Without pitch or oakum there was nothing to be done about the deck, and the sprung beam could not be repaired, but Mr Fitton cut down the rig from felucca to lugger, using the off-cuts for patches sewn in position with twine obtained by ravelling down the remnants of canvas. Scarcely had they got the ship re-rigged and everything embarked than so fierce a squall blew up that both cables parted, leaving the little ship with no means of anchoring.

Undismayed, Mr Fitton made for Cartagena, intending to cruise from there along the coast as far as Portobello in the expectation of capturing some sort of vessel which might take them to Jamaica. When nearing Cartagena a Spanish coast-guard schooner approached, the *Santa-Maria*, armed with six long 6-pounders and ten swivels, with a complement of 60 men. The ships were quite close when Mr Fitton screwed up his one gun and began an engagement which lasted half an hour, the lugger making up for the disparity in guns by its greater weight of shot and the celerity with which the gun was served. They fired round-shot and grape alternately, the Spaniard apparently incurring many casualties, until she broke off and made for the island of Varus. The lugger tried to grapple her without success, and both ran ashore at the same time, within ten yards of each other. Without hesitation Mr Fitton sprang overboard, and with his sword in his teeth swam to the Spaniard, followed by all of his men who were fit; they swarmed up the side and after a short fierce encounter carried the schooner.

Once again Mr Fitton had captured a vessel of three times his gun-power and twice his manpower, for almost half of his 45 men were sick. His casualties were two killed and five wounded, the Spanish five killed and nine wounded, including the unfortunate commander, Don Josef Coréi, who had both hands shot off together. A most creditable little victory, and Mr Fitton found himself in command of two ships; but unfortunately both were fast ashore, while the local Spaniards were gathering and commencing musket fire. It soon became clear that it would be impossible to get the Spanish schooner off, so they took the anchors and cables out of her to haul off the lugger; but before this could be done they had to throw overboard their one gun – indeed its supporting beam was so strained that it could never fire again. Once afloat they took all the stores from the schooner, set all the prisoners ashore dead or alive, set fire to the ship and made off, as anxious to avoid an enemy as they had been to encounter one. In four days they reached their base, with no food or water left, no prizes, and only a splendid little victory to their credit.

The captain and the commander-in-chief did justice, and at long last the coveted commission came through, and it was Lieutenant Fitton who commanded the flag-ship's tender. By January 1805 this was the schooner GIPSY, with ten 4-pounders and 45 men. She was sent by the commander-in-chief to deliver despatches to the PRINCESS CHARLOTTE, 36-gun frigate, Captain Gardner, the rendezvous being off Cape Antonio. While hanging about there the GIPSY was chased by five privateers, two schooners and three feluccas, and at once made out to sea in the hope that they would separate in the chase and give a chance of capture. This did happen; the larger of the schooners outsailed all her consorts such a distance that the GIPSY was able to tack towards her and engage her in a running fight; so much to the disadvantage of the Spaniard in attempting to escape she ran on the Colorados reef and became a total loss. Misliking what they saw, the rest made off under all sail and were not seen again. The GIPSY remained on her station for three days until the PRINCESS CHARLOTTE came up, and Lieutenant Fitton was able to hand his despatches to Captain Gardner.

The exploits of Fitton and his 45 men, as they fought their way up from an open boat to a 10-gun schooner, may seem a chronicle of very small beer; but the merit of an action depends in no way on the numbers engaged. The story demonstrates once again how a compact body of daring and resolute men, well commanded, can triumph again and again against apparently impossible odds.

17

The Pelican

The PELICAN was one of the first 18-gun brig-sloops to be fitted out with sixteen 32-pounder carronades and two long 6s, giving her quite a broadside at close range. She was commanded by John Clarke Searle, an excellent officer, with a usual complement of 121 men and boys, whom Searle had worked up into a very good crew indeed. In 1796 she was cruising in the West Indies and took some prizes, which had to be given prize-crews to take them to Jamaica, so that by 23rd September she had only 97 of her crew on board when she sighted a large sail to windward. This was soon made out to be a French frigate of the 36-gun class, in fact the *Médée*, mounting 40 guns altogether, and with a crew of about 300 men – about three times the PELICAN in tonnage, gun-power and crew. Commander Searle judged it prudent to take evasive action, but the *Médée* was much the faster ship, and overhauled rapidly; flight was therefore impossible, and it was either fight or surrender. Thinking he perceived a certain wavering among the men, Commander Searle called them aft and assured them that if they carried out his orders exactly as they had always done, they would at least beat off the frigate if not take her. The men gave him a cheer, cleared for action and shortened sail to fighting rig.

As the frigate approached, she opened fire; but the brig did not return this until the two ships were close enough for carronades, when her first broadside killed the man at the wheel, wounded three others, and disabled a gun. The cannonade went on furiously for nearly two hours, during which the PELICAN was damaged about the spars and rigging but had only one man slightly wounded. At length the *Médée* turned away, exposing her stern for a moment, when the PELICAN was able to put in a raking broadside, causing further damage and casualties, which now amounted to 33 killed and wounded. The *Médée* now fairly made off for Guadeloupe, and the PELICAN was in no condition to follow; well content with having beaten off her big opponent, she set to repairing the damage.

This was at 9 a.m. At 10 a large sail was reported, and by 11 the PELICAN was able to make sail in chase, overtaking at 3 p.m. This was the ALCYON, a British store-ship, which had been captured by the *Médée* a few days before and was now re-taken by the PELICAN. She was taken in tow, but the wind fell away to a dead calm while there was still a heavy swell on the sea, so she was cast off and the two ships drifted about on the swell all night.

Dawn found them fairly near the coast of Guadeloupe, near the French naval harbour of Anse-le-Barque, the ALCYON much closer inshore than the PELICAN; there was also descried the *Médée* at anchor within gun-shot of the ALCYON. She now got out her boats and soon re-took the store-ship, while the PELICAN, helplessly becalmed, could only look on. The morning breeze off the land now came up, and another frigate came out of Anse-le-Barque to stand by the *Médée*, so Commander Searle judged it prudent to use the same breeze to go off to the nearby Iles des Saintes, then in British occupation.

The French captain was so impressed by the 32-pound shot from the PELICAN that he reported that he had been engaged with a frigate which had had her mizzen mast removed; sufficiently improbable that the Governor of Guadeloupe actually sent an ADC to the Saintes under a flag of truce, to enquire about the vessel. This was a fine vindication of the

policy of arming these small ships with heavy carronades, proving to the whole Royal Navy that a brig so armed could actually
take on a frigate, given the right officers and men. There was
no prize to show, however, and no special recognition was made
by Admiralty, although Searle was made post quite shortly
after.

In 1797 the PELICAN was still in the West Indies, with the
same well-trained crew, but now under Commander John
Gascoyne; he, however, fell ill and had to be put ashore, the
command devolving on Lieutenant Thomas White. Cruising
off San Domingo, a strange brig was sighted approaching from
northward, the wind being east. The PELICAN went to meet her
hoisting British colours, on which the approaching brig hoisted
French. She was the privateer *Trompeur,* with twelve long
6-pounders and 78 men, not really a match for the PELICAN;
but she had a consort at a little distance, a schooner with 60 men.
As they passed each other both opened fire; the PELICAN swung
neatly round the stern of the *Trompeur,* giving her a raking
broadside, continued round and came up close alongside within
most effective carronade range. It would have been better tactics
for the Frenchman to have stood off to try the long-range
effect of his long 6-pounders, but the ships kept up a close and
furious action for more than half an hour, the French captain
plainly seen on the quarter-deck encouraging his men, who
stood to their guns like heroes.

Now the schooner came up, and her large crew could be seen
assembling on deck with the evident intention of boarding the
PELICAN on her disengaged side. To be boarded on both sides
is a very awkward situation: Lieutenant White gave up hope
of capturing the French brig, and determined to get her out of
the way. Approaching even closer, he ordered the muzzles of
the carronades to be depressed, so that the 32-pound shot
went through her side and bottom. At the third broadside she
went down by the head and sank in five minutes. The schooner
now put about and went off to windward; instead of chasing
her, which would probably have been unsuccessful, Lieutenant

White got out his boats and was able to save 60 Frenchmen, including the gallant captain, so that only 18 were lost. The PELICAN had one killed and five wounded.

Without the intervention of the schooner, the result of the meeting would not have been in doubt. Lieutenant White showed great judgment and resolution in destroying the brig before he could be assailed by superior numbers, and once again he demonstrated the mighty fire-power of 32-pounder carronades, properly handled.

A well-built wooden ship lasts a long time. Ships which fought the Armada were still in the line of battle under Blake, so it was not surprising that the PELICAN was still in service in 1813, after twenty years of warfare. She was now commanded by John Fordyce Maples, cruising in home waters. On the 12th August 1813 she came into Cork for stores and re-fitting, but within an hour she was out again, beating against a half-gale. The American brig *Argus* was actually in St George's Channel, capturing and burning all the shipping she met. Next day at evening a fire was seen, and a brig standing away to the SE. The PELICAN went in chase, but lost sight after nightfall. Early next morning the same brig was seen, having just set another ship on fire, and now making for a group of merchant ships. There was no doubt that this was the *Argus*, and the PELICAN made after her with all sail; nor was there any attempt to escape, for her Captain William Henry Allen was anxious to try his ship against a British brig. The two were a fair match, the *Argus* having eighteen carronades, 24-pounders, and two long 12s, with a remaining crew of 125 men.

At six that morning, St David's Head in sight about fifteen miles to the east, the ships drew alongside, hoisted their colours and opened fire. With her veteran crew, the fire from the British brig was for once superior to the American. In less than five minutes Captain Allen was mortally wounded, and the command fell to Lieutenant William Henry Watson, who handled her with great skill despite the serious damage to her spars and rigging. The PELICAN now sought to cross the stern of the *Argus,* but was prevented by adroit manoeuvring. After the carronade had continued for twenty minutes the *Argus* was so much damaged as to be practically disabled; the PELICAN was now able to cross her stern, raking her from stern to stem with her heavy 32-pound shot, and then came round on her starboard quarter. Passing up her broadside, the PELICAN grappled at the bow and immediately boarded. There was very little resistance, and the American colours came down after a fight of three-quarters of an hour.

The PELICAN had two killed and five wounded, and was so slightly damaged that she was perfectly fit to fight the battle all over again. The *Argus* had 14 killed or mortally wounded, and another 14 wounded. Although seriously damaged, she was temporarily repaired and sent into Plymouth under command of Lieutenant Thomas Welsh of the PELICAN, with all the wounded and a half of the prisoners, while with the other half Commander Maples proceeded to Cork to make his report to Admiral Thornborough. Captain Allen of the *Argus* died at Plymouth and was buried with all honours.

This engagement was received with great approval in Britain. The succession of American frigate victories had been broken in March by the victory of the SHANNON, but the presence of American sloops in home waters had caused considerable alarm, particularly among overseas traders and their insurers, who were greatly comforted by the decisive defeat and capture of the *Argus.* It was observed that at least some of the defeats could be put down to recently constructed ships and raw crews, whereas when a veteran crew which had long served together under the same command, as in the SHANNON and now the PELICAN, met a ship of equal force it was victorious. The shaken belief in the British invincibility on the seas, the faith of all men's childhood, was restored.

18

The Hornet

Shortly after the declaration of war in 1812, the government of the United States decided to send a squadron into the Pacific, consisting of two frigates and a sloop, which was almost a quarter of the whole available American Navy. The story of the two frigates has already been told (*The Frigates,* Chapters 13 and 15), but the sloop also had a varied and adventurous career.

The BONNE CITOYENNE, 20-gun post-ship, Captain Pitt Barnaby Greene, was on a voyage from the River Plate with coined silver to the value of £500,000; grounding on a shoal off the east coast of Brazil in mid-November, she put into the port of Salvador (Bahia) for repairs. Early in December the 44-gun big American frigate *Constitution* and the 18-gun sloop *Hornet* arrived off the port, waiting to pick up their consort the *Essex*, frigate, for their projected cruise. While time hung heavy, the *Hornet* sent in a challenge to the BONNE CITOYENNE to come out and fight, the *Constitution* promising not to interfere. This Captain Greene very properly declined: if he were victorious, it was very unlikely that the great *Constitution* would really see her consort taken clear away as a prize without happening to fall in with them a day or two later; and Captain Greene's duty was to get his much-needed coin to England, whatever scrap was offered. The two sloops were very nearly a match, the American being a trifle heavier in gun-power and number of crew.

The *Essex* did not arrive; the *Constitution* went off and sank the JAVA, and then had to go home for repairs; which left Captain James Lawrence in the *Hornet* to wait for the BONNE CITOYENNE to come out, or whatever might turn up. What did turn up was the MONTAGUE, 74, Captain Manley Hall Dixon, and the *Hornet* had to carry out some very neat evading action to save herself from this line-of-battle ship. Having got clear away she made for the Caribbean, while the MONTAGUE escorted the BONNE CITOYENNE on the next stage of her important voyage, leaving Salvador on the 26th January 1813 and arriving at Portsmouth in good time for her cargo to help to pay the armies which were closing in on France.

The *Hornet* picked up some prizes on the Caribbean coast, and on the 24th February sighted a British brig at anchor among the shoals at the mouth of the Demerara River, making repairs to her rigging. This was the ESPIEGLE, 18-gun brig, Commander John Taylor. She was temporarily incapable of movement, but to get at her the *Hornet* had to make a wide sweep round the sandbanks; and while doing so came across yet another British brig, the PEACOCK, Commander William Peake, sixteen carronades, 24-pounders, and two long 6s. Both ships were seen from the ESPEIGLE until about 1 p.m., when they were manoeuvring for the windward gauge, and went out of sight to the SE. The ESPIEGLE, in no great haste to get her rigging completed, made no attempt to come to the aid of her consort, and next day went into the port of Demerara, for which Commander Taylor was afterwards court-martialled. He was lucky to be acquitted on the capital charges, being merely reprimanded for not having exercised his men sufficiently at the guns; so it was perhaps well for him that he did not engage the expert gunners of the *Hornet*.

The PEACOCK was the smartest sloop in the Royal Navy. Her paintwork was perfection, her spars shone with varnish, her deck was holystoned snow-white, every piece of brass sparkled, every carronade was black-leaded and oiled, even their breech-ropes were encased in pipe-clayed canvas. The only thing odd about her guns was that they were never fired – a smoky messy business at the best.

After the usual manoeuvring for the wind, the two sloops passed each other on opposite tacks, exchanging a broadside as they passed. Unfortunately the first broadside left the PEACOCK almost unarmed on the larboard side: some of the carronades overturned; some drew the fastenings from the ship's side; some of the breeching-ropes broke, rotten under their pipe-clayed sleeves. The PEACOCK wore around to come up again with her starboard side to the enemy, possibly with some hope that this side might be better; the *Hornet* ran in close on the PEACOCK's starboard quarter and in a quarter of an hour reduced her to flinders. Her commander and four others were killed and 33 were wounded; her mainmast was down, and she had six feet of water in the hold; not only were her colours down, but she hoisted an ensign upside down on the foremast as a signal of distress. The *Hornet* had one killed and two wounded, plus two seriously injured by an accidental explosion.

No time was lost in getting out boats, nor was any effort spared to save the ship and crew they had so skilfully defeated; but she was going too fast, and even while they were throwing overboard the beautifully polished guns, she sank straight down in 33 feet of water, so that her foremast stood up like a beacon. Three Americans and four of the PEACOCK's men saved themselves by clinging to the foretop until they were rescued; the American lieutenant and his men were able to jump into their boats just in time; four of the PEACOCK's men took a small boat and made off in the confusion, ultimately making their way into Demerara; probably about five were drowned. Had it not been for the promptitude and efficiency of the *Hornet*'s men in coming to the rescue, very few of the PEACOCK's crew could have been rescued.

The *Hornet* had a slight advantage in weight of broadside and number of crew, but as usual the difference was qualitative:

K

it was a battle between expert gunners and skilled valets, between a strongly built well-practised ship of war and a light vessel fit for any review. Had the PEACOCK had the commander and crew of the REINDEER, of exactly the same force, she would indeed have put up a fight, but probably not with success. Apart from the splendid fighting efficiency of the ship, great courage was shown by the *Hornet* in engaging a sloop apparently her equal while there was another a few miles away which might be expected to come into action with all speed; but even if the ESPIEGLE had come in, with her equally un-practised crew, it is unlikely that the two together could have met the devastating fire of the *Hornet*. It was perhaps as well for British *amour propre* that the ESPIEGLE had a pressing engagement in Demerara.

Perhaps the greatest single difference between the times we are speaking of and today is in communications. Nowadays any event of any importance is known throughout the world within minutes of its occurrence; Napoleon had the same means of communication as Alexander of Ashurnasirpal – horse and sail.

Land communications could be improved by road-making and organisation, but over the oceans wind, weather and accident ruled supreme. The news of Nelson's decisive victory at Aboukir was of the most urgent importance, but it was not received in London until exactly two months later. Thus con-ferences rolled on for months after the events of war had negated their terms of reference, and war continued uselessly after peace had been declared. Having said all this, it is still difficult to justify the American government in despatching a squadron to the Pacific on 20th January 1815. Peace had already been signed at Ghent on the 24th December 1814, and while it is probable that the government did not know this, they certainly knew that negotiations were well advanced and that a peace was absolutely essential : America's overseas trade had been annihi-lated,* cutting off her sole source of revenue, the Customs, and

* See Appendix 2.

the states of Massachusetts and Connecticut were preparing to secede from the Union and make a separate peace. In such circumstances, to despatch a squadron to the Pacific, whence it could not be recalled for many months, was the action of reckless desperadoes rather than a responsible government.

The squadron consisted of the *Peacock* (of which more later), the *Tom Bowline*, brig store-ship, and the *Hornet*, now commanded by James Biddle who, as a lieutenant, had hauled down the colours of the FROLIC when she was captured by the *Wasp* (1). The first rendezvous in case of separation was Ascension Island, then uninhabited,* and as the store-ship sailed rather slowly the *Hornet* pushed on ahead to reconnoitre the situation at Ascension, a frequent sighting-point for vessels from India to Britain. It is said that on the 20th March Commander Biddle was informed by 'a neutral' that peace had been signed three months before; this is very possible, but actual evidence is lacking.

The PENGUIN was an 18-gun brig, very much the same as those already described, with sixteen 32-pounder carronades and two long 6s; hastily constructed under contract the previous year and manned by excellent officers, but with a crew which could only be described as the sweepings of the receiving ships. The commander, James Dickinson, had been first lieutenant of the frigate CERBERUS in the glorious action off Lissa, told elsewhere (*The Frigates*, Chapter 12), and had been promoted commander thereafter. He had an excellent lieutenant, MacDonald, and good warrant and petty officers, but his crew were very mixed : some young 'quota men', some very old re-pressed men (some over 70 years of age) and 17 young boys. With this lot Commander Dickinson was sent out to the Cape; while there, the local C-in-C, Vice-Admiral Tyler, had in-formation of the American privateer *Wasp* (page 179) as having been seen on the India trade route, and sent Dickinson out in search; drafting him, however, twelve Marines out of his

* Ascension was first garrisoned by Britain in 1815, as part of the elaborate arrangements for Napoleon, on St Helena.

flag-ship, showing exactly what he thought of the manning of the PENGUIN.

Patrolling on the line Cape of Good Hope–St Helena–Ascension, the PENGUIN came across the *Hornet* off the north end of Ascension, the limit of her beat; the British vessel had had no news of peace and, coming up, hoisted her colours and fired a gun as a demand to the stranger to show hers. This she did, passing on the opposite tack and firing a broadside, to which the PENGUIN replied, with the same wretched result as on her former consorts, that many of the carronades upset or tore away from the bulwarks. Any apprentice artificer nowadays knows that the same bolt-mounting which is rock-firm in oak will tear right through pine, but the same fittings had been accepted : an extra inch on the outer bolt-plate would have made all the difference. This action continued for about half an hour at a range of fifty yards when the *Hornet* fell away a little, and Commander Dickinson, seeing that gunnery could accomplish nothing, prepared to board. Before he could give more than the preliminary orders he fell, mortally wounded, but Lieutenant MacDonald carried out his intentions. The PENGUIN ran on board the *Hornet*, with her bowsprit between the *Hornet*'s after rigging, but then it broke, bringing down with it the PENGUIN's foremast with all its sails, blanketing the forward guns, while the after ones had been mostly dismounted. In this situation, and having no colours left flying, Lieutenant MacDonald hailed the *Hornet* that he was surrendering.

The PENGUIN had 10 killed and 30 wounded out of her 105 men and 17 boys. The *Hornet* out of her 163 men and 2 boys had 2 killed and 11 wounded, according to her report; but according to the British prisoners, losses were actually heavier, some killed having been put overboard before the British prisoners were brought aboard : certainly the proportion of killed to wounded is unusual for American reports. Immediately after the surrender the *Peacock* and the store-ship came up, and whatever news they had heard there was eagerness to pursue the Pacific voyage; so next morning the PENGUIN was fired and the American sloops proceeded on their way.

Not, however, for long. On 28th April, in the South Atlantic, halfway between Tristan da Cunha and the Falklands, they came in sight of what they took to be a fat East Indiaman, and immediately bore down in chase. What they hoped to devour was in fact the CORNWALLIS, 74, Captain John Bayley, with the flag of Rear-Admiral Sir George Burlton, KCB. The American sloops had never dreamt of meeting a line-of-battle ship in the roaring forties, and were quite close in before they discovered that they had made an error; they separated in flight, the *Peacock* going off to the SE, and the *Hornet* northwards, which ship the Rear-Admiral chose to chase. All day the pursuit continued, the battleship gaining, until she had to heave-to in order to drop a boat for a Marine who had fallen overboard. The remarks of the Rear-Admiral have not been recorded. Up again, on again, off again, the chase continued for two more days, the CORNWALLIS showing a remarkable turn of speed for her class; perhaps the Rear-Admiral had discarded some of the tons of guns on her upper-works, which were quite superfluous for her present work. The *Hornet* threw away her anchors, then her boats and spare spars, then her bell and forge, then her cables and her small arms, and finally all her guns and shot. In the long run she got away, and in fact made her home port, but no longer as a ship of war.

19

A Swarm of Wasps

The ostensible reasons why the United States of America declared war on Britain in 1812 had to do with stopping American ships to search for deserters, impressing American subjects, and the declaration of a general blockade of Europe; all matters which could very well have been settled by negotiation, and in fact were twice so settled, but first one side and then the other refused to ratify the agreement. The underlying reasons may have been territorial: America was always expansionist, like Russia; she had recently acquired the vast southern territories of Florida and Louisiania from Napoleon for dollars down, and may now have been looking northwards to Canada. Thirty years before, the Republic had won independence by a combination of several European powers against Britain; now that most of Europe was combined under Napoleon against Britain, might not Canada join the Union? Furthermore, since the French cruisers had been practically swept from the seas, great and rich British convoys were traversing the Atlantic with no other escort than a single frigate or sloop, to scare off casual pirates: handsome pickings.

To occupy Canada by land seemed a feasible enterprise, but to challenge Britain on the sea appeared the utmost temerity. The United States' whole Navy consisted of 8 frigates and 12 sloops, not a single line-of-battle ship; whereas Britain had at sea in full commission 102 line-of-battle ships, 124 frigates and about 400 sloops. In the outcome the land attack on Canada was totally unsuccessful, whereas at sea the American warships had an unbroken succession of victories for the whole of the first year.

The reasons were not far to seek. In the first place, the overwhelming Royal Navy was not there; almost the whole of its main strength was tied up in blockading Napoleon's fleets in the various European ports. It was the old story of the cat at the mousehole; the mouse can't get out, but the cat can't go away; so it is just as much a prisoner as the mouse. In this case it was a mighty dangerous mouse: outside Toulon lay Vice-Admiral Sir Edward Pellew, with sixteen ships of the line and three frigates, blocking Vice-Admiral Emeriau, with eighteen or twenty ships of the line and eight frigates. This situation was repeated all round the coast of Europe : it was impossible to slacken the blockade to provide even a few heavy ships to deal with a handful of frigates and sloops on the other side of the Atlantic. Let the frigates and sloops on the American stations get on with it.

This is where the second circumstance came into play : in almost every case the American vessels were larger, stronger and better built, better armed and far better manned than their British nominal counterparts. There were no rules governing the various types of ships, although the rigs were closely defined. Thus a sloop was a ship-rigged three-master, but might be almost any size consistent with the rig, so long as it was definitely smaller than the smallest frigate in its navy. A brig must always be two-masted and square-rigged, a schooner two-masted and rigged fore-and-aft; but there were no limits on size. Thus the British regarded a schooner as one of the very smallest warships, meant for winkling petty pirates out of their hidey-holes in the West Indies. Quite a large class of British schooner was 75 tons, with four 12-pounder carronades and 20 men and boys; while the Americans, with their incomparably greater experience of this rig, built schooners of well over 300 tons, with at least ten long 12-pounders and more than 100 men. During the war the new American sloops were of 540 tons British measure, about 100 tons larger than the largest British sloop.

As for building, the British sloops varied greatly, the best being those which had been captured from the French. Home-built ones were mostly run up by contract in yards used to building merchant ships, in contrast to the frigates and ships of the line, which were always built in the Royal Dockyards to the highest standards. For cheapness and speed the sloops were often, at this stage of the war, built of pine and other light timbers. The Americans, on the other hand, had a continent of splendid ship-timber to choose from, and only the best was chosen. During the whole period of building an experienced captain supervised the work, with full powers to reject anything not perfect. The timbers and planking throughout were much heavier, the masts and yards far stouter, than in the equivalent British ships.

The American Navy was by far the best-manned of the period, the nearest in quality being the Danish (at this time including Norway). While the British had to use the press-gang and the quota system, and the French were conscripting peasant boys, the Americans were accepting only the best of the volunteers. The New England states produced a race of mariners equal to the best in the world, and in addition they had a valuable stiffening of experienced men-of-war in the form of deserters from the Royal Navy (page 41). In general the American naval officers were all native born, but a large proportion of the petty officers and senior ratings were British. These could be relied upon to the last; they would never surrender of their own accord, for to be taken in arms against their native country was certain death.

It was this qualitative superiority of the individual American ships that was not understood, or at least not acknowledged, by Admiralty, and many a ship and many a man were lost before the lesson was learnt.

The name *Wasp* has long been honoured in the Navy of the United States, and is at present carried by one of the most powerful ships in the world. At the period of the 1812 war it was a small-ship cognomen, and to make things easier for the meticulous student it was borne by three quite different ships in one year.

The 18-gun British brig-sloop FROLIC, Commander Thomas Whinyates, had a long five-year tour of duty in the Caribbean during which she was sorely stricken with malaria, which seriously debilitated the survivors, amounting to 92 men and 18 boys. This extraordinary proportion of youngsters was owing to two reasons: the great difficulty in scraping a crew together, and the fact that the West Indies had been cleared of all French ships of war, and the only danger was an occasional small privateer or pirate, very unlikely to try conclusions with an 18-gun brig. It was with pleasure that the order was received to quit this pestilential climate and escort a convoy of fourteen merchantmen from Belize, British Honduras to England.

For sailing ships at that period the route from the Caribbean, after clearing the islands, was north on the wind and current, keeping west of the Sargasso weed, and picking up the southwester between 30° and 40° north latitude, according to the season. Commander Whinyates – but we should call him Captain, for he was gazetted post captain on 12th August 1812, although he did not know it for many months – sailed with his convoy from Belize on 12th September 1812, rather close to the hurricane season. Off Havana he spoke an outward bound Channel Island ship and was informed that the United States had declared war on 18th June, three months before, and had already captured the 38-gun British frigate GUERRIERE on 19th August 1812 (*The Frigates,* page 144–5). This was doubly bad news: although it was well known that the Americans had three big frigates, it was not believed that one of them could force a British 38-gun frigate to surrender; and if such was the fighting capacity of the Americans, Captain Whinyates could not but reflect that, with his weakened crew and tethered to his convoy, he would have little chance against a freshly outfitted American sloop of about his own gun-force; and yet he could not honourably avoid it.

The weather was rough, and before clearing the islands the FROLIC sprung her fore topmast. On the night of the 16th October, about 200 miles north of Bermuda, a hurricane scattered the convoy, sprung the main topmast of the FROLIC, carried away her main yard, and tore her sails badly. She hove-to all next day and night in a confused high sea to make what repairs were possible and to allow her convoy to rejoin her. Six of them did so before dark on the 17th, and at dawn on the 18th another sail was seen approaching and thought to be another of the convoy, until she failed to reply to the recognition signal. Ordering the convoy to make the rest of its way on its own, the storm-battered FROLIC turned to meet the approaching enemy, setting what sail she could. It was not much, with no main yard and with both topmasts sprung: a reefed topsail on the fore yard and her driver; enough to give her steerage way to steady her somewhat in that horrible sea, tossing from every direction.

The enemy was the 18-gun ship-sloop *Wasp*, Captain Jacob Jones, armed almost exactly as the FROLIC, with sixteen carronades, 32-pounders, and two long guns: 12-pounders in the *Wasp* and 6s in the FROLIC: There was nothing much to choose either in tonnage or weight of broadside; the difference was in fitness, of ships and of crews. The *Wasp* had a crew of 168 men, like their ship in perfect condition, five days out from Delaware Bay; the FROLIC had been five years in the West Indies, carried 92 men and 18 boys, almost all reduced in health, and the ship was so damaged that she had only two spars left on which to set sails.

Before the storm Captain Whinyates had sighted a Spanish brig-of-war escorting a Spanish convoy, and the possibility existed that they had also been seen from the *Wasp*; the FROLIC therefore hoisted Spanish colours in the hope of delaying, for the benefit of her convoy, the inevitable combat. The *Wasp* approached within sixty yards and then hailed; immediately the FROLIC hoisted British colours and opened fire with musketry as well as guns; the *Wasp* replied at once, closing the range. Although there was little wind, the sea was so tumultuous that on both sides the muzzles of the carronades were often under water.

The first ten minutes of battle were very much to the FROLIC: inside five minutes the *Wasp*'s main topmast came down, and a few minutes later the mizzen topgallant mast and the gaff of the driver. Had the FROLIC been fully rigged this would have given her a possibly decisive advantage; as it was, the most that offered was a chance to escape, and now this too was lost; a shot carried away the peak halyards, down came the gaff and with it the driver, leaving the FROLIC with no means of movement whatever, a mere hulk tossing on the seas.

The *Wasp* now took up an advantageous position across the FROLIC's bow, whence she was able to rake the brig from bow to stern with only one gun able to reply. This cannonade went on for half an hour, the FROLIC obstinately keeping her colours flying, until at last the *Wasp* came alongside and boarded without resistance, finding practically nobody alive on the deck except the man at the wheel and three wounded officers, including the captain. Lieutenant James Biddle of the *Wasp* now cut down the FROLIC's colours, which at the fall of the gaff had been lashed to the mainmast.

In all encounters between British and American ships the casualties were dreadfully heavy: both sides fought with the same tactics, the same principles of gunnery, and the same grimly tenacious courage. In this case the FROLIC was so shattered that both her masts went overside a few minutes after her surrender; she had 15 killed and 47 wounded, so that more than half her crew were casualties. The *Wasp* had the spar damage described, and her losses were eight killed and eight wounded.* Captain Jones has been criticised for prolonging the cannonade instead of boarding to finish the action with less loss

* It is to be observed that British casualty reports almost always show the wounded as more than twice the killed, whereas American reports show the numbers about equal. The reason is that the British sailor got 'smart money' for any wound he reported to the surgeon; in American ships this did not apply, so that the captain usually reported as wounded only those actually incapacitated.

of life, but it was no part of his duty to save the lives of the enemy so long as their flag flew; it was perfectly open to Captain Whinyates to stop the slaughter at any time by hauling down his colours, which he would have been perfectly justified in doing any time after the gaff fell and left the ship immovable.

There was little enough time given to either to exult or deplore. During the afternoon, while the two ships were lying together, the line-of-battle ship POICTIERS, Captain John Poer Beresford, came up and took them both without resistance, the spar damage to the *Wasp* making escape impossible. Captain Beresford very properly retained Captain Whinyates in command of the FROLIC. In due course he stood court-martial for the loss of his ship and was most honourably acquitted; indeed, it was his determined resistance and the damage inflicted on the *Wasp* which made possible the capture of that ship, which could otherwise have easily sailed away from the heavy 74.

Very different was the treatment of Captain Jones, although he came home without either his own ship or his prize. He and his crew received the thanks of Congress along with a present of 25,000 dollars, a gold medal for the captain and silver ones for all the officers: such is the enthusiasm of a young nation in the early stages of a popular war.

When it finally penetrated to Admiralty that the three American big frigates were superior in every respect to any British frigate afloat, steps were taken to 'abate the nuisance', among others the provision of really powerful fast ships. The smallest class of 74-gun line-of-battle ship was obsolescent, all were more than twenty years old; the Navy had started the wars with 54 of them, and there were still 20 left. Three of these, the MAJESTIC, SATURN and GOLIATH, were drastically cut down by removing poop, quarter-deck and forecastle; freed of all this superstructure and the 22 guns carried thereon, but retaining the full sail power of the 74, it was hoped that they would be as fast and as handy as the American big frigates. For armament they retained the lower battery of twenty-eight long 32-pounders, and on the upper deck mounted twenty-eight large carronades, 42-pounders, with two long 12-pounder chase guns. They were rated as 56-gun ships, but were much larger and more powerful than the earlier ships of the same rating, which were East India ships bought into the service. Thus fitted and armed, with excellent crews and experienced captains, they went forth seeking what they might devour.

On 2nd February 1814 the MAJESTIC, Captain John Hayes, was cruising in the Atlantic about a hundred miles east of the nearest of the Azores when a ship came in sight to windward bearing down towards her. This was the American privateer *Wasp*, from Philadelphia, of 20 guns, which at first mistook the MAJESTIC for a large Indiaman and scented a rich prize, but finding the mistake in good time made off to the NE under all sail. The MAJESTIC made after her, hoping she might be the big frigate *Constitution*, which was known to have sailed from Boston a month before. After chasing all night, at dawn she was within four miles of the *Wasp* and gaining when there appeared to the southward, about ten miles off, a squadron of two large frigates, another ship and a brig. This seemed a likelier proposition, and the MAJESTIC went off in chase of the two frigates, which turned out to be 40-gun French frigates, of which the MAJESTIC ran down and captured one; but the *Wasp* got clear away.

In 1813 three American sloops were launched, rated as 18-gun sloops, mounting twenty carronades, 32-pounders, and two long 18-pounders; these were larger than any previous sloop, being 540 tons (English measure) and carrying 175 men. Apparently to confuse future students, but possibly for some other reason known to themselves, these sloops were named *Frolic, Peacock* and *Wasp*.* They were intended for long-distance cruising.

The REINDEER, 18-gun brig-sloop, Commander William Manners, was by no means the best of her class. She

* For elucidation, see Appendix 3.

had been run up of fir, quickly and cheaply under contract, during the invasion scare of 1803–5. She was intended to carry 32-pounder carronades, but after a few years these were exchanged for 24-pounders, sixteen of which, with two long 6s, was as heavy an armament as her timbers could carry. Of 385 tons, she carried a crew of 98 men and 20 boys. They had the advantage of long service together in the sloop, under the same commander, who had worked them up into a splendid crew who simply idolised their handsome, young and aristocratic commander. On account of this happy and united complement, the REINDEER, in her base town, was called the 'Pride of Plymouth'.

In June 1814 the REINDEER was cruising in the Western Approaches, about 500 miles west of Ushant. Trade was slack, for the war in Europe had ended; Napoleon was on Elba, and Allied armies had restored Louis *le gros* to his acquiescent subjects. The only war was with the United States, and the vast power of the Royal Navy was now available to crush that minor flotilla. The odd privateer might be picked up and there were rumours that some of the sloops had sailed with stores for a long cruise, but the big American frigates were all in their home waters.

At dawn on 28th June, with the wind light from the NE, a sail was sighted in the WSW, and the REINDEER went in chase to investigate; the ship was in fact the *Wasp* already described, commanded by Johnstone Blakeley, intent on bringing the war right to Britain's doorstep. A daring feat, this was made possible by the fact that the great fleets had been withdrawn from the Scheldt, the Channel and off Brest; some to be laid up, some to be paid off, and a few to go to American stations; so that there was some scope for bold raiders, although nothing like serious warfare could be undertaken.

As the REINDEER came up, the chase was recognised as one of the new large sloops, far more than a match for the brig; nevertheless the chase was continued, both ships trying for the weather gauge, at which the REINDEER was successful, and the action began about 3 p.m. A close and furious cannonade was kept up on both sides for more than half an hour, supplemented, on the American side, by a rapid and accurate musketry from the fighting-tops. Commander Manners was shot through the calves of both legs, but kept the deck. One of his men had a strange and fearful wound: an American Marine, in haste, left his ramrod in his musket, and this, fired at short range, transfixed the skull of a gunner; he went below to have the protruding shaft sawn off for convenience, and returned to his gun. After the action the rest of the ramrod was removed, and the heroic gunner made a complete recovery.

The REINDEER was now so battered as to be quite unmanageable, and she came against the *Wasp* with her bow against the enemy's larboard quarter, in such a position that she could be raked both by cannon and musketry, with very little capacity to reply. Most of the officers were down; the commander was again shot through both thighs, which knocked him down, but he sprang up again to lead his men in the only possible desperate attempt. 'Follow me, my boys, we must board her!' and, blood pouring from his wounds, leapt into the rigging to lead aboard, when two bullets from the *Wasp*'s maintop struck him through the head, and he fell back dead on his deck. The *Wasp*'s crew now boarded in their turn, and with their overwhelming numbers rushed the ship to the quarter-deck, where they received the surrender of the vessel from the commander's clerk, Mr Richard Collins, the senior man left on his feet.

What the *Wasp* had captured was a wreck and a shambles. Of her crew of 98 men and 20 boys, the REINDEER lost 25 killed and 42 wounded, most of them seriously; above the waterline, she had had been simply shot to pieces, although both masts were still standing, tottering. Seldom has a ship lost half her complement in half an hour, and such destruction shows the efficiency of the *Wasp*'s commander and crew. Out of 173 men and 2 boys she lost 11 killed and 15 wounded, showing the fight that the REINDEER's men had put up against odds which perhaps her commander should not have challenged;

but such amazing victories as that of the SPEEDY over the *Gamo* had given an unfounded idea of British superiority, and they had to find out the hard way that American ships and American crews were every bit as good as their British equivalents, and in many respects decidedly better.

The two ships lay together overnight, but in the morning the foremast of the wreck fell, and Commander Blakeley decided that she could never be made seaworthy; so taking out the wounded and prisoners he set her on fire, and made for Lorient, where he lay for almost two months repairing and refitting.

This very long repose in Lorient is a very odd thing, diplomatically. Britain and France were not only at peace but in alliance; the King of France had been for more than twenty years an honoured guest in Britain, and owed his restoration in great part to British tenacity; yet an enemy warship, after destroying a British ship, was allowed to enter a French port, land his wounded and prisoners, and enjoy every facility to refit in order to pursue the war. Stranger still, the British did not station a frigate off the port to intercept the *Wasp* when she came out. There may, indeed there must, have been some diplomatic accommodation, for when the *Wasp* emerged she had given up the idea of raiding in British waters and laid a course for home.

The 18-gun brig, such as the REINDEER, was something the Royal Navy was not short of: from two in 1793, the class had grown to 81 at the beginning 1814. The standard armament was sixteen 32-pounder carronades and two long 6s, although in the case of the REINDEER the armament had to be lightened. On the 1st September 1814 the AVON, of this class, Commander the Hon. James Arbuthnot, was cruising about between Madeira and Casablanca, at the time sailing SW with the wind fair from the SE. As darkness was falling she was overtaken by a strange ship on much the same course; this was in fact the *Wasp*, so little expected that more than two hours were spent on night signals and hailing until the AVON was satisfied that this was an enemy, and it was after 9.30 p.m. that she opened with her broadside, without much effect, the standard of gunnery being wretchedly bad. Not so with the *Wasp*: her first broadside cut the peak halyards of the AVON, letting the big driver sail fall over the after guns and blinding them; the next broadside brought down the mainmast, blinding most of the other guns with sails and wreckage, and leaving the AVON unmanageable and unable to make any effective reply to the rapid and accurate fire of the *Wasp*.

The AVON had nothing left standing from which to show her colours, so about 10.30 p.m. the *Wasp* ceased fire and came close, hailing to know if she had surrendered; the answer was 'Yes'. The *Wasp* now hove-to in order to take possession of her prize when she became aware of another sail coming up. This was the brig CASTILIAN, Commander David Braimer, a sister ship of the AVON. Recognising the situation, she opened fire on the *Wasp*, which did not reply but made off downwind under all sail, pursued by the CASTILIAN; but the AVON now made signals of distress and her sister ship turned back to her rescue. At midnight she got out her boats and took off the AVON's crew; no sooner was this completed, in about an hour, than the AVON heeled and sank, illustrating her determined resistance to the last and also the devastating fire of the *Wasp*. She had 10 killed and 32 wounded out of her complement of 104 men and 13 boys, including all her commissioned officers.

The *Wasp* did not appear to have much damage, and was out of sight when day broke. On the 15th September she was spoke off Madeira, but was never seen again: presumed foundered with all hands. The loss of the gallant ship was mourned not only in America but in Britain, where the daring audacity of her cruise had been widely admired by open-minded people, much as the cruise of SMS *Emden,* Captain Müller, in the Indian Ocean, exactly a hundred years later.

L

20

The Last Shots: Tragedy of Errors

In almost all wars, once the issue is no longer in doubt, there is noticeable a certain disinclination for heroic action on both sides, particularly among the victors. Nobody wants to get himself killed on the last day of a war, however valiant he may be and however fiercely he may have fought when his country was in jeopardy. Thus the last shots of a great war tend to be random and sporadic; yet those mopping-up operations are just as necessary and dangerous as the great decisive actions. Montaigne remarks, 'A man is not always on the top of a breach, or at the head of an army in the sight of his general, as upon a scaffold. A man is oft surpris'd between the hedge and the ditch, he must run the hazard of his life against a hen-roost, he must bolt four rascally musketeers out of a barn.'

On 12th March 1814, as the Allied armies were gathering around Paris, the 18-gun ship-sloop PRIMROSE, Commander Charles Phillott, was lying-to about a hundred miles west of Coruña, on the lookout for anything passing Cape Finisterre. At 2 in the afternoon, wind NE by E, a sail was reported to leeward, standing SW; she was observed to alter course more to the westward, avoiding the PRIMROSE, and sail was made in pursuit. What she was chasing was in fact the British packet brig DUKE OF MARLBOROUGH, from Falmouth to Lisbon with the mails and some military passengers. The trouble was that each mistook the other for an American privateer, or even a naval ship, because of the impression made by the incursions of the Americans into the Western Approaches. It was like the expectation of German parachutists in Britain in 1940; far from panic, or even alarm, but inducing an exaggerated state of suspicion and readiness.

About ten miles away the PRIMROSE fired a gun and hoisted a small blue ensign at the gaff, and when within seven miles hauled this down and put up a larger red ensign. It is unlikely that these could be distinguished at that distance, and if they had been they would have been ignored. The conventions of war at that time permitted the use of false colours up to the very moment of opening fire, and an American privateer in those waters was more likely to use British colours than any others. Then the business of hoisting first a blue ensign and then a red was exactly what one might expect of an American privateer, who could not be sure of the currently acceptable ensign. The DUKE OF MARLBOROUGH hoisted the private recognition signal, but her flags were much smaller than usual for King's Ships, and as she was dead ahead of the PRIMROSE and the wind almost astern, the flags streamed out ahead and could not be made out. Obviously this was another privateer ruse; after two hours the DUKE OF MARLBOROUGH, having had no answering signal, hauled it down, sure that she was being pursued by an enemy, and prepared for battle, fetching two long brass 9-pounders aft to her stern ports. As it came dark the commander of the packet, who had the well-known name of John Bull, ordered the private night recognition signal to be made, but nobody was quite sure what that was; and whatever signals were made, the PRIMROSE made no reply.

The wind now freshened, and the bigger ship began to overtake quite rapidly, at which the DUKE OF MARLBOROUGH opened fire with her stern chasers, doing some damage to the headsails and forward rigging of the PRIMROSE, which made no reply; but coming up on the starboard quarter, both the commander and the second lieutenant (who had Stentor's voice) hailed. Whether

The Last Shots: Tragedy of Errors 163

both ships hailed together and confused the sound, or whether the distance was too great, the only reply was by gunfire, which killed three men and wounded three. The PRIMROSE now began to fire as her guns could be brought to bear, but Commander Bull manoeuvred his ship with such skill that she suffered no damage. The PRIMROSE now ran upon her opponent's quarter, intending to board, but Bull had run out a spare spar as a boom, so that his big antagonist could not get aboard of him. At the same time the fire of the packet's stern guns still further damaged the sloop's rigging, and she had to fall away to re-fit. Coming up again on the beam, she was able to bring her broadside to bear, and the DUKE OF MARLBOROUGH ceased firing, on which Commander Phillott hailed again to know if she surrendered, and found out, to mutual consternation, that the fight was between allies.

Under other circumstances Commander Bull would have had great credit for the masterly manner in which he defended his ship against hopeless odds; he had two passengers killed, including the adjutant of the 60th Regiment, and about ten wounded. The ship was much damaged, had three and a half feet of water in the hold, and was practically sinking from heavy shot through the hull below the waterline. She was saved by the carpenter of the PRIMROSE and his mates coming on board to plug the shot-holes. The PRIMROSE had three killed and twelve wounded, and suffered moderate damage to her spars and rigging. Both commanders would have deserved praise had they been in fact engaged with an enemy; as it was, it may be imagined that they wrote up their logs and reports with something less than rapture. It was, however, neither the first nor the last time that so disastrous an error was made.

During the Hundred Days, while Napoleon's veteran soldiers flocked to rejoin his eagles, there was no such enthusiasm in the French Navy. Napoleon had not led *them* to victory after astounding victory; he had not made *their* leaders dukes and princes; and his severity towards unsuccessful naval officers was notorious. He refused to take wind and weather into account, just as he had done during his Moscow campaign. Moreover, the long years cooped up in harbours had as always sapped the morale. Still, there were captains who were proud to hoist the tricolour again, and one of these was Capitaine de fregate Nicholas Touffet, commanding the corvette *Légère*, twenty carronades 24-pounders, two long 12-pounders, and four 6s on the quarter-deck. She sailed from Toulon and about fifty miles west of the northern tip of Corsica fell in with the brig-sloop PILOT, Captain John Toup Nicolas, sixteen carronades 32-pounders and two long 6s, on the 17th June 1815, while a wet and weary British army was taking up positions in front of the village of Waterloo.

There was the usual manoeuvring to get the weather gauge, in which the PILOT was successful, coming up abeam about 2.30 p.m., when both ships hoisted their colours and the PILOT fired a single shot through the corvette's foresail. The *Légère* replied with a broadside, and the cannonade began; as usual, the French firing high at the rigging, the British firing low at the hull and the men. This went on for about an hour and a half, when the French fire became intermittent and random; shortly she was seen to back some sails in order to drop astern. The PILOT tried to do the same, but her rigging was so much cut up that she was unable to do so and could only keep on ahead. Wearing with the wind, she tried to cross the bows of the *Légère* and rake her, but immediately the corvette hauled as close to the wind as possible and made off to windward under all sail, leaving the PILOT virtually disabled for sailing. The crew set to work with a will, however, and within an hour had some sail set and went in chase, making more repairs en route. By this time the *Légère* was six miles off, with her rigging in good order, so the chances of catching her were slim; however, the PILOT chased all night, but in the morning there was no sign whatever of the *Légère*.

The casualties on board the PILOT amounted to 2 killed and 14 wounded; but those of the *Légère*, out of a much larger crew of probably 170 men, have been given as 22 killed and 78 wounded, which would indeed have given her good reason to flee from a much smaller ship. The PILOT was fought in a way to do every credit to her commander and crew, but it does not appear that much notice was taken of the action, since by the time the report reached Britain all attention was focused on Paris, where on 7th July Wellington marched in triumphantly at the head of a British Army, the first for 400 years. It is not enough to fight a fine action: it is necessary to do it at the right time.

I have already animadverted on the recklessness of the American government in despatching a squadron to the Pacific when they knew that peace negotiations were well advanced, the peace having in fact been signed a month before the squadron sailed. The only ship to get out of the Atlantic was the *Peacock,* 18-gun ship-sloop, Captain Warrington; without touching at the Cape she made her way across the Indian Ocean, making for the Sunda Straits, a fine locality for picking up richly-laden Indiamen. She hove-to off Anjier (now Anjer Lor) where the East India Company maintained a station, and where was lying one of the Company's armed ships, the NAUTILUS, ten carronades and four long 9s, Lieutenant Charles Boyce. He sent out a boat with his sailing master and an officer passenger to enquire if the American sloop had heard that peace had been declared on 24th December of last year, it being now 30th June 1815; and at the same time the Company's harbourmaster went out in his boat, with a copy of the declaration of peace signed by Mr Madison, which he had been given by an American merchant ship which had called. When the two officers from the NAUTILUS came on board they were instantly hustled below; when Mr MacGregor, the harbourmaster, came aboard he had time to show the declaration to the first lieutenant and the purser before he too, on the captain's order, was taken below.

These proceedings had been observed from the NAUTILUS, which now came alongside, and Lieutenant Boyce hailed Captain Warrington to ask him whether he knew that peace had been declared six months ago. The only answer he received was a brusque order – 'Haul down your colours instantly!' In view of the overwhelming superiority of the *Peacock* it would have been as well if Lieutenant Boyce had complied under the strongest protest, and it is difficult to see what Warrington could have done next. He could not long have pretended ignorance of the peace, and that any act of war was now piracy, a hanging matter; moreover the 22-gun VOLAGE, which had fought a frigate at the battle of Lissa, was approaching the straits with excellent means of persuading Warrington to keep the peace. However, Boyce refused, and the *Peacock* opened fire; the NAUTILUS replied, wounding five men, but shortly had such a fearful casualties for so small a ship that she hauled down the flag – of the Honourable East India Company, not a Royal Navy ensign.

The casualties the NAUTILUS suffered by this atrocity were dreadful: six killed, her commander frightfully wounded, her lieutenant mortally wounded and seven others wounded. Lieutenant Boyce had a large grape-shot through his hip, and his leg smashed by a 32-pound shot; he survived in great pain, but had to have his leg amputated at the hip and was of course crippled for life. His First Lieutenant Mayston lingered for five months after the action before he died. Wounds and death are inevitable in war, and every fighting man steels himself both to inflict or to receive; but so much the more does every fighting man abhor wanton slaughter. The NAUTILUS was a Company's ship, reporting to the Governor, and the news did not reach England for a long time, when the government was engrossed with post-war problems; but no doubt if the NAUTILUS had been a King's Ship, Admiralty would have pressed the government to insist on Captain Warrington being hanged, even if it meant renewing the war – which might have been not a bad thing to relieve the political situation at home.

These were the very last shots of the wars, which have never been renewed, although most early Victorian politicians and historians considered their renewal inevitable, and gave very convincing reasons for their predictions; but Time has his own way of dealing with prophecy. At the present time it is quite impossible to visualise Britain at war with either France or the United States under any circumstances whatever. That is a certainty. But I remember hearing in the House of Lords the late Duke of Bedford, an ardent pacifist, say to the House, 'You have had your way; you have totally destroyed your enemies : have you no enemies left?'

Glossary

ABACK: sails are aback when the wind is pressing them against the masts. To be taken aback; to find the ship unexpectedly in such a position, usually unmanageable.

ABAFT: towards the rear of the ship.

ABEAM: on one side of the ship, especially when the main-masts are in line.

ABOARD: any part of any deck of a ship, inside the hull. 'Come aboard' is the usual invitation into the ship. 'To run aboard' usually means an accidental collision.

ADRIFT: a ship without use of her sails, anchors or boats, drifting about with the winds and currents.

ALOFT: anywhere in the ship higher than the main-masthead.

ANCHORS: the best bower is stowed at the cat-head nearest the bow on the starboard; the second bower in the same position on the larboard; the sheet anchors are stowed immediately aft of these; all four anchors are of the same size and weight, usually 4 to 5 tons in ships of the line, and about $1\frac{1}{2}$ tons in a sloop. The kedge anchor is usually lighter and has more than two flukes, being intended to drag off a ship that has run aground or is otherwise helpless.

BACK: a wind backs if its apparent source changes in a counter-clockwise direction.

BEATING: proceeding to windward in zig-zag fashion, each of the beats as close to the wind as the vessel will sail.

BAR: a shoal to be expected across the mouth of a river.

BRACES: ropes fastened to the yardarms for the purpose of swinging and fastening them.

BOW: the most forward part of a ship's hull. An object is reported to be 'on the bow' if it lies within 45° of the line to which the bow is pointing.

BINNACLE: the strong box built immediately forward of the wheel to contain the compass, lights, etc.

CABLE: the heaviest rope on the ship, being the thick strong rope by which the anchor is attached, usually made up in lengths of 120 fathoms.

CAT-HEADS: the short strong beams projecting from the forecastle, to which the anchors are made fast.

CLEW: the lower corner of a square sail or aft corner of a fore-and-aft sail.

CLEW-EARRING: the loop by which the clew of the sail is made fast to the yard.

CLOSE-HAULED: sailing as close to the wind as possible.

CRANK: unstable in the hull, requiring great care to prevent capsizing.

DRIVER, or spanker: the largest fore-and-aft sail on a full-rigged ship, spread by boom and gaff on the mizzen mast.

FISH: to repair a spar by lashing smaller timbers strongly around it.

FLEET: more than ten warships under a single command. See 'squadron'.

HEAVE-TO: to check the movement of a ship by setting one or more of its sails aback (q.v.).

KNOT: a denomination of speed, signifying one nautical mile per hour; measured at this period by heaving over the stern a log attached to a knotted cord, the number of knots being counted while a sand-glass was running, the knots being 50·57 feet apart for a 30-second sand-glass.

LARBOARD: the left side of a ship when looking forward; now called 'port'.

LATEEN: a large triangular sail set on a long sloping yard; a favourite Mediterranean rig, especially for smaller ships.

LIE-TO: having hove-to (q.v.), to continue to lie with as little motion as possible by adjusting the sails.

LOOM: an indistinct appearance, at night or in fog.

MUSKET-SHOT: an inexactly estimated distance, usually taken as 200–300 yards.

MIZZEN: the aftermost mast of a ship having more than two.

OFFING: in the vicinity. In the case of land, at a safe distance offshore. In the case of a vessel, within topmast sight but well out of shot.

PINTLE: the bolt by which the rudder is attached to the stern.

PISTOL-SHOT: an estimated distance, usually taken as about 50 yards.

QUARTERDECK: that part of the ship's deck, usually raised, extending from the mainmast to the stern. Reserved for officers, except for ratings on duty.

RAKE: to cannonade the whole length of a ship, either from astern or forward.

SLIP THE CABLE: to allow the whole of the cable to slip through the hawsehole, having attached a buoy by a rope longer than the depth of water, so as to pick it up later. To be distinguished from CUT the cable, when the cable is cut through with axes and the anchor abandoned.

SPLICE: to unite two ends of rope by twisting the strands together.

SPRING: when anchoring with a spring, a rope is passed out of a stern-port and passed forward, where it is made fast to the anchor ring. After the anchor has taken hold, the ship may be swung in any direction by means of the spring rope.

SPRING: a spar is sprung when it has partially split longitudinally.

SQUADRON: a number of warships less than ten, under one command. See 'fleet'.

STARBOARD: the right-hand side of the ship, looking forward.

STAYS: a ship is said to be in stays when the sails are temporarily aback when changing course.

TACK: tacking is used in the same sense as beating (q.v.), but is also applied to each straight course between changing direction: e.g. a ship beating to windward might make long tacks so as to keep as great an area as possible under observation, or she might make short tacks so as to arrive sooner at her destination.

WEATHER: the weather side of a ship is that from which the wind is blowing.

WEATHER-GAUGE: to be on the weather side of an enemy, almost always a tactical advantage.

WAY: a ship is under way when it is moving through the water under full control. Steerage way is just enough movement to allow the rudder to do its work.

WEIGH: to pull up the anchor. If more than one anchor is down the ship is 'moored' and has to be brought to a single anchor before she can weigh.

Notes on the Plates

Jacket illustration Probably a convoy collecting in the Downs; more probably for the West Indies than the East. The Deal galley punt in the left foreground was the principal ship-to-shore boat, and was remarkably weatherly. All detail is remarkably accurate in this oil by Brooking.

Plate 1 The French chasse-marée was the pest of the English Channel. With her enormous sail-power and her large crew of skilled Breton mariners, she could run away from anything more powerful and capture any merchantman. On this occasion she has come rather close inshore to pillage and fire a merchantman, and the brig is going to get her in this weather.

Plate 2 The SCOURGE and the *Sans-Culotte*. This was the first action of the war. The British brig, half-gunned and with 20 less than her complement, engaged the French privateer *Sans-Culotte*, and after a battle of three hours captured her and brought her into port. See Chapter 3.

Plate 3 The ANTELOPE and the *Atalante*. The ANTELOPE, carrying mails in the West Indies, was intercepted by the much larger *Atalanta* and actually brought her as a prize to Jamaica. The drawing, unfortunately, is by no means a model of correctitude. See Chapter 3.

Plate 4 The VIPER. A remarkable class of ship intended especially for the carrying of despatches in all weathers. Note the four rows of reefing points. She could also carry another large jib and a large square-sail on her topmast. See Chapter 8.

Plate 5 The WOLVERINE. An experimental type of vessel, she gave an excellent account of herself off the French coast, and was eventually sunk in a magnificent but hopeless action in the Atlantic, which allowed her convoy to escape. See Chapter 11.

Plate 6 Aristocratic Captain. Thomas, Lord Cochrane, in the full uniform of a captain at the age of 27. The worthiest successor of Nelson, he fell foul of Authority. See Chapter 4.

Plate 7 Plebian Captain. James Cook, greatest of all navigators, in the uniform of a lieutenant, to which he had just been promoted, at the age of forty, in order to command a ship of war, and map the world.

Plate 8 The *Wasp* and the REINDEER. There were a number of *Wasps* in the American Navy, which are elucidated in Appendix 3. The last *Wasp* made a daring sally into the English Channel and sank two British brigs under the noses of the Channel Fleet. This *Wasp* was lost with all hands on the passage back to America. See Chapter 19.

Plate 9 The *Hornet* sinking the PEACOCK. Immediately after the PEACOCK surrendered, both ships anchored in 33 feet of water, and the PEACOCK hoisted a flag of distress, correctly shown as the ensign upside down. She sank in minutes, but the prompt action of the *Hornet*'s boats saved all but five of the survivors. The action took place much further from the shore than depicted. Four British sailors made off in a boat (eventually reaching Demerara) and these are seen in the middle distance. The brig on the extreme right is the ESPIEGLE, among the sands off the mouth of the Demerara River; as shown, the position agrees with most American accounts, but in the shallow water the foretop of the PEACOCK stood up for years, and subsequent survey showed her to be at least 20 miles from the nearest possible position of the ESPIEGLE.

Effect of Cannon Fire on Wind

Ever since the introduction of cannon as the main weapon of naval warfare it had been noticed that light breezes died away to a calm when a cannonade was opened. This happened so often that it was accepted by all naval authorities as axiomatic. Later generations, which did not use the wind for propulsion and were accustomed to a few high-velocity guns per ship, have been inclined to criticise this as merely empirical and capable of other explanation. For a light wind to die away to a calm is nothing unusual, with or without a cannonade, and cordite in rifled guns produced no perceptible effect on the wind. It is, however, to be explained theoretically as well. Smooth-bore guns used enormous quantities of propellant—15 pounds for a 32-pound shot, 4 pounds for a 4-pounder; a big ship like the VICTORY would blaze off a quarter of a ton of powder in a single broadside, while two sloops alongside firing at each other would be discharging a hundredweight of powder a minute into the confined space between the ships. This produced enormous quantities of hot gases, causing an area of comparatively high atmospheric pressure around the ships, quite enough to nullify any slight wind pressure.

Effect of the War on American Trade

All expressed in terms of current pounds sterling

Year	Total exports	Total imports
1807	£22,571,488	£28,869,765
1812	8,026,506	16,047,916
1814	1,443,216	2,701,041

British Trade in the Same Years

1807	£31,015,526	£26,734,425
1812	38,041,573	26,163,431
1814	53,573,234	33,755,264

M

Elucidation of the Sloop Names
Frolic, Peacock and Wasp

FROLIC. Brig-sloop, 18 guns actual, Commander Thomas Whinyates. 384 tons. Captured 18th October 1812 by *Wasp* (1) and recaptured the same day by POICTERS, 74.

Frolic. American sloop, ship-rigged, 18 guns nominal, 22 actual, Commander Joseph Bainbridge (*not* Commodore Bainbridge of the *Constitution*). 509 tons English measure. Launched early in 1813, first of the three. No particular history. Captured 20th April 1814 between Cuba and Florida by the frigate ORPHEUS, 36 guns nominal, Captain Hugh Pigot, and the 12-gun schooner SHELBURNE, Lieutenant David Hope.

PEACOCK. Brig-sloop, 18 guns actual, Commander William Peake. 386 tons. Captured and sunk 24th February 1813 by the American ship-sloop *Hornet*, Captain James Lawrence (Chapter 19) off Demerara.

PEACOCK. Ship-sloop, 18 guns nominal, probably 24 actual, Commander Richard Coote. Foundered at sea with all hands, Northern Caribbean, August 1814.

Peacock. American ship-sloop, 18 guns nominal, 22 actual, Commander Lewis Warrington. 509 tons American, 540 tons English measure. Launched early 1813. Several successes (Chapter 19). Penetrated the East Indies, and on 30th June 1815 engaged and captured the Honourable East India Company's 10-gun schooner NAUTILUS, Lieutenant Boyce, unfortunately some months after peace had been declared. Survived the war.

Wasp. American ship-sloop, 18 guns actual, Commander Jacob Jones. 434 tons. Captured FROLIC (see above and Chapter 18) and was the same day captured by the POICTERS, 74, 18th October 1812. Taken into the Royal Navy as LOUP-CERVIER; served on the American coast. Foundered with all hands 1815.

Wasp. American privateer, 20 guns actual, of Philadelphia. Chased off Azores by the MAJESTIC, Captain John Hayes, 2nd and 3rd February 1814, but escaped.

Wasp. American ship-sloop, 18 guns nominal, 22 actual, Captain Johnston Blakeley. 509 tons American, 540 tons English measure. Launched early in 1813. Conspicuously successful in several courageous actions. Last sighted 15th September 1814 off Madeira, returning to US after a most creditable cruise in British waters. Foundered at sea with all hands, latter half of September 1814 (Chapter 18).

TABLE I

Strength of the Royal Navy in sloops, brigs, etc. in 1793 and in 1814

The following classes commanded by a Commander

	1793	1814
Ship-rigged sloop, quarter-decked, 18 guns		33
flush-decked, 18 guns		7
quarter-decked, 16 guns	13	10
flush-decked, 16 guns		3
quarter-decked, 14 guns	7	
Brig-sloop, 18 guns	2	81
16 guns	5	32
14 guns	7	14
10 guns		28
Bomb-ketch, 8 guns and 2 mortars		8

The following classes commanded by a Lieutenant

	1793	1814
Gun-brig, 14 guns		3
12 guns		67
10 guns		1
Cutters and Schooners (all fore-and-aft rig)		
14 guns	11	8
12 guns	6	8
10 guns		24
8 guns		2
6 guns		1
4 guns	1	10
Totals	52	340

This table refers only to ships in full commission.
Omitted are all ships in reserve or under repair, armed transports and storeships, and all ships, armed or not, which had not the primary purpose of seeking battle with the enemy.

The gun-force given is the nominal rating; in the case of the larger sloops the actual force was greater; see Chapter 1.

TABLE II

Losses of the Royal Navy, for the years 1793 to 1815 inclusive, in the classes of vessels named in Table I

Year	By enemy action	By perils of the sea
1793	2	3
1794	6	3
1795	2	2
1796	1	10
1797	2*	8
1798	3	6
1799	2	7
1800	1**	10
1801	5	6
1802†	none	2
1803§	2	5
1804	5	9
1805	5	14
1806	7	10
1807	9	19
1808	11	15
1809	4	21
1810	1	8
1811	7	9
1812‡	4	14
1813	7	12
1814	7	13
1815	2	5
Totals	95	211

Grand total 306

*One ship lost by crew mutinying and taking ship into enemy port.
**Lost by crew mutinying and taking ship into enemy port.
†Peace of Amiens ratified 10th October 1801.
§War resumed 18th May 1803.
‡After this date, most losses by enemy action were to American ships.

TABLE III

Sloops and brigs, etc. of the Royal Navy, lost by foundering or capsizing at sea between 1793 and 1815 inclusive

Year	Name	British-built or captured	Guns	Area where lost	Fate of crew
1794	Actif	captured	10	West Indies	all saved
	Spitfire	captured	6	West Indies	all lost
1796	CURLEW	British	18	North Sea	all lost
	SCOURGE	British	16	North Sea	all saved
	Bermuda	captured	14	West Indies	all lost
	HELENA	British	14	North Sea	all lost
1797	SWIFT	British	18	China Seas	all lost
	Vipere	captured	16	West of Ireland	all lost
	Hermes	captured	16	uncertain	all lost
	Pandora	captured	14	North Sea	all lost
	RESOLUTION	British	14	uncertain	all lost
1798	Braak	captured	16	Delaware Estuary	35 lost
1799	Orestes	captured	18	Indian Ocean	all lost
1800	Chance	captured	18	uncertain	25 saved
	Trompeuse	captured	18	English Channel	all lost
	Railleur	captured	14	English Channel	all lost
1801	Babet	captured	20	West Indies	all lost
	Utile	captured	16	Mediterranean	all lost
1802	Scout	captured	18	North Atlantic	all lost
	FLY	British	14	North Atlantic	all lost
1803	CALYPSO	British	16	West Indies	all lost
	AVENGER	British	14	North Sea	all saved
1805	Hawke	captured	18	English Channel	all lost
	Imogene	captured	18	West Indies	all saved
	Orquixo	captured	18	West Indies	95 lost
	SEAGULL	British	18	uncertain	all lost
	Redbridge	captured	10	West Indies	all saved

182

Year	Name	British-built or captured	Guns	Area where lost	Fate of crew
1806	MARTIN	British	18	West Indies	all lost
	SERPENT	British	18	West Indies	all lost
	SEAFORTH	British	14	West Indies	only 2 saved
	CLINKER	British	12	off Havre	all lost
	Papillon	captured	10	West Indies	all lost
1806	*Berbice*	captured	4	West Indies	all saved
1807	BUSY	British	18	North Atlantic	all lost
	PROSPERO	British	Bomb-ketch	North Sea	uncertain
	SPEEDWELL	British	14	English Channel	uncertain
	Elizabeth	captured	12	West Indies	all lost
	Fire-fly	captured	12	West Indies	only 4 saved
	CASSANDRA	British	10	North Sea	all saved
	Maria	captured	10	West Indies	all lost
1808	TANG	British	8	West Indies	all lost
1809	LARK	British	18	West Indies	only 3 saved
	FOXHOUND	British	18	North Atlantic	all lost
	HARRIER	British	18	East Indies	all lost
	CONTEST	British	12	North Atlantic	all lost
	PELTER	British	12	West Indies	all lost
	Dominion	captured	14	West Indies	only 3 saved
1810	SATELLITE	British	16	English Channel	uncertain
	CONFLICT	British	12	Bay of Biscay	uncertain
1811	FANCY	British	12	Baltic	all lost
	Fleur-de-la-Mere	captured	10	North Atlantic	all saved
1812	*Magnet*	captured	16	North Atlantic	all saved
	NIMBLE	British	10	Kattegat	all saved
	CHUBB	British	4	North Atlantic	all lost
	PORGY	British	4	West Indies	all lost
1813	SARPEDON	British	10	West Indies	all lost
	RHODIAN	British	10	West Indies	all saved
	SUBTLE	British	10	West Indies	all lost
1814	ANACREON	British	18	English Channel	uncertain
	Peacock	captured	18	West Indies	all lost
	CRANE	British	18	West Indies	all lost
	Vautour	captured	16	uncertain	all lost
	Dart	captured	10	uncertain	all lost
	CUTTLE	British	4	North Atlantic	all lost
	HERRING	British	4	North Atlantic	all lost
	Elisabeth	captured	10	North Atlantic	uncertain

Total of sloops, brigs, etc., lost by foundering at sea 66

Of these, total British-built 36

Of these, total captured previously from enemy 30

Areas in which lost	Number of ships
West Indies	26
North Atlantic	13
North Sea	7
English Channel	7
Eastern waters	3
Baltic and Kattegat	2
Delaware Estuary	1
Mediterranean	1
Uncertain	6
	—
	66

Losses of crews	Number of ships
All lost or 4 or less saved	48
All saved	9
Heavy loss	3
Uncertain	6
	—
	66

INDEX

Names of British vessels are in SMALL CAPITALS, names of other ships are in *italics*.
Abbreviations: Adm—Admiral; Cmdre—Commodore; Cdr—Commander.